J.K. LASSER'S

How to
PAY LESS TAX
on Your
RETIREMENT
SAVINGS

J.K. LASSER'S

How to
PAY LESS TAX
on Your
RETIREMENT
SAVINGS

Seymour Goldberg, CPA, MBA, J.D.

Macmillan • USA

Macmillan General Reference
A Simon & Schuster Macmillan Company
1633 Broadway
New York, NY 10019

Copyright © 1995 by Seymour Goldberg

A J.K. Lasser Book

J.K. Lasser and Macmillan are registered trademarks
of Simon & Schuster, Inc.

Goldberg, Seymour, 1913–
    J.K. Lasser's how to pay less tax on your retirement savings/
Seymour Goldberg.
        p.   cm.
    Includes index.
    ISBN 0–02–860088–6
    1. Old age pension—Taxation—Law and legislation—United States—
Miscellanea.   2. Individual retirement accounts—Taxation—Law and
legislation—United States—Miscellanea.   I. Title. II. Title: How
to pay less tax on your retirement savings.
KF6425.Z9G64   1995
343.7305'24—dc20
[347.303524]   95–46623
                                                        CIP

Manufactured in the United States of America

10 9 8 7 6 5 4 3 2 1

Contents

Introduction

As the population of the United States ages, the need for retirement distribution planning becomes vital. Many taxpayers have accumulated a significant amount of assets in retirement type accounts during their working careers through their participation in qualified corporate plans, Keoghs, 403(b) plans, IRAs, and other similar plans. Unfortunately, many individuals with considerable retirement plan assets are unaware that substantial tax burdens may await them or their beneficiaries when distributions commence.

There are many IRS rules applicable to distributions from retirement plan accounts. Some rules apply while you are alive and other rules are triggered on your death. If you have a working knowledge of these rules then both you and your family can take advantage of them in a manner that can result in a substantial tax savings for the entire family. Too many taxpayers have not done any tax planning with their retirement funds. The goal of this book is to help you understand the distribution rules for IRAs and employer retirement plans so that you can maximize their tax-saving potential and avoid unexpected tax burdens for yourself and your heirs.

This book is written in question-and-answer format. The questions and answers emphasize not only the many IRS rules but also tax planning strategies and income tax deferral techniques. For example, several chapters in this book emphasize techniques in passing your retirement assets to children and grandchildren in order to preserve the tax deferred growth of your retirement assets for decades after your death. Another chapter deals with preserving your retirement assets for your surviving spouse, explaining what your spouse must do after you pass away in order to further protect your retirement assets for the family. This book does not include questions and answers on excess annual distributions during your lifetime or the special excess retirement accumulation tax that can apply to your estate, as these apply only in rare cases involving very substantial retirement assets.

The questions in this book are based on real-world situations. The answers are based upon the author's actual experiences as well as his analysis of IRS rules. In many cases, detailed computations are provided to illustrate in dollars-and-cents how the distribution rules apply in actual situations. Special emphasis is placed on IRA distribution planning. Although the required distribution rules for qualified employer plans and IRAs are generally the same, distributions from qualified employer plans are frequently transferred to IRAs, requiring the IRA owner to take tax-planning steps. Do not consider this book a substitute for a professional advisor. Your professional advisor, whether an accountant, attorney, or financial planner, must be involved in creating and implementing your retirement distribution plan. Your professional advisor can also keep you informed about changes in the tax laws that could affect the distribution rules and planning techniques described in this book.

If you are interested in receiving information on other publications or products regarding retirement distributions, please write to:

Seymour Goldberg

c/o J.K. Lasser Institute

1633 Broadway, 7th Floor

New York, NY 10019

CHAPTER 1

Tapping Your Retirement Plan Savings without Penalty Prior to Age 59½

Many taxpayers wish to withdraw funds from a qualified plan, 403(b) annuity or IRA, prior to age 59 ½ without being subject to a 10% early distribution penalty which may apply to the taxable portion of the distribution. The reason for tapping retirement funds prior to age 59 ½ will vary from taxpayer to taxpayer. Several reasons include the need to pay for a child's college, purchase of a house, loss of a job, or having excessive retirement plan savings. Despite these needs the taxpayer may discover that some retirement plans do not allow early withdrawals.

The following questions and answers illustrate the application of the 10% penalty. Not all distributions before age 59 ½ are subject to the penalty. There are exceptions that apply to IRAs as well as to employer plans, but some exceptions are not available to IRAs. Note that Congressional legislation could affect the penalty rules. For example, when this book went to press, Congress was considering a proposal to establish a new type of nondeductible IRA, from which penalty-free distributions could be made to buy a first home or to pay for qualifying higher education costs or medical expenses.

There is also a 15% penalty on excess distributions. You should consult your professional advisor about potential liability for this penalty, which applies to an IRA owner or plan participant (but not beneficiaries) to the extent that distributions exceed an annual floor, which for 1996 is $155,000 or $775,000 for a qualifying lump-sum distribution eligible for special averaging.

Question 1.1: *Does the 10% early distribution penalty apply to distributions from all retirement plans?*

Answer: The 10% penalty applies to early distributions from all "qualified retirement plans." This includes IRAs, simplified employee pensions, pension plans, profit sharing plans, stock bonus plans, annuity plans, and 403(b) annuity contracts.

Question 1.2: *Assume that Carol Jones attains age 59 on January 15, 1999 and 59 ½ on July 15, 1999. If Carol receives a distribution of $10,000 from her IRA on July 14, 1999, is she subject to a 10% early distribution penalty?*

Answer: Yes. She is subject to a 10% early distribution penalty of $1,000, equal to 10% of the $10,000 distribution, since she received a distribution prior to attaining age 59 ½. If Carol is in the 28% tax bracket she will pay $2,800 in income tax (28% × $10,000) plus $1,000 for the early distribution penalty. Distributions received on or after July 15, 1999 would not be subject to the early distribution penalty because Carol will then be at least 59¹/₂ years old.

The Rollover Exception to the Penalty:

A qualifying rollover of a distribution from an employer plan to another employer plan, or to an IRA, avoids tax on the distribution and also the 10% penalty for early distributions. Rollovers from one IRA to another are also tax free and penalty free.

Question 1.3: *Carol Jones receives an IRA distribution of $5,000 on February 1, 1998, when she is age 58. She rolls over $5,000 into another IRA on March 15, 1998. Is Carol subject to a 10% early distribution penalty?*

Answer: No. The 10% early distribution penalty is not applicable if Carol rolls over the $5,000 IRA distribution into another IRA within 60 days from the date of receipt of the distribution. The 10% early distribution penalty is based upon the amount reported as taxable income on the recipient's income tax return. If the IRA distribution is timely rolled over, then it is not subject to federal income tax and therefore will not be subject to the 10% early distribution penalty.

Question 1.4: *If Carol had timely rolled over to another IRA only $2,500 of the $5,000 IRA distribution in Question 1.3, what would the tax and penalty be?*

Answer: Since $2,500 was not timely rolled over, $2,500 would be taxable to Carol. She would also pay a penalty of $250, equal to 10% of the $2,500 taxable distribution.

Question 1.5: *How often can you roll over distributions received from an IRA?*

Answer: According to the IRS you can receive a distribution from an IRA and roll over all or part of it into another IRA only once in any one-year period.

Question 1.6: *Assume that you are not age 59 ¹/₂ and have more than one IRA. Can you receive and roll over a distribution from each IRA during a given one-year period without being subject to the 10% early distribution penalty?*

Answer: The law is not clear on the subject. However, the IRS in Publication 590 (1994 version) and in Letter Ruling 8731041, dated May 6, 1987, has taken a liberal position and states that the one-year rule applies separately to each IRA that is maintained by an individual.

IRS Publication 590 (1994 version) provides as follows:

> You can take (receive) a distribution from an IRA and make a rollover contribution (of all or part of the amount received) to another IRA only once in any one-year period. The one-year period begins on the date you receive the IRA distribution, not on the date you roll it over into another IRA.
>
> This rule applies separately to each IRA you own. For example, if you have two IRAs, IRA-1 and IRA-2, and you roll over assets of IRA-1 into a new IRA-3, you may also make a rollover from IRA-2 into IRA-3, or into any other IRA within one year after the rollover distribution form IRA-1. These are both rollovers because you have not received more than one distribution from either IRA within one year. However, you cannot, within the one-year period, again roll over the assets you rolled over into IRA-3 into any other IRA.
>
> If you violate the rules described above and receive another distribution from an IRA within a one-year period, then such distribution will not qualify as a rollover. Such additional distribution is taxable and is subject to the 10% penalty on early distributions.

Question 1.7: *If you receive a distribution from an IRA, may you roll it back into the same IRA within the 60-day period instead of into a new IRA?*

Answer: Yes. The IRS issued Letter Ruling 9010007, dated December 14, 1989, which stated the following:

> ...IRA distributions are tax free in the year of distribution if the rollover rules...are met. As long as the IRA distribution is redeposited into the same or another qualifying IRA within 60 days of receipt of the distribution, such distribution would constitute a qualified rollover.

The letter ruling also stated the following:

> The individual may make such a rollover of a distribution only once a year.

Question 1.8: *Instead of receiving a distribution from my IRA, and making a rollover within 60 days, can't I switch IRA investments by asking one IRA trustee to make a direct transfer to another IRA trustee?*

Answer: Yes. By authorizing a direct transfer of your IRA, you can make a tax-free transfer without having to handle the funds yourself. A direct transfer also has this advantage: you are not subject to the once-a-year limitation on rollovers (Questions 1.5 and 1.6).

If you are under age 59½, the 10% early distribution penalty does not apply to a direct transfer because there is no taxable distribution.

Question 1.9: *Arthur Anders leaves his job with XYZ Corp. in 1998 at age 52 and joins another company. He is entitled to a $100,000 lump-sum distribution from his 401(k) plan account at XYZ Corp. Can Arthur avoid the 10% early distribution penalty on the lump sum by making a rollover?*

Answer: Yes, a rollover can avoid both tax and penalty, but to avoid withholding, Arthur should instruct the XYZ Corp. plan administrator to make a "direct rollover" to an IRA that he designates, or to the plan of his new employer.

If the distribution is paid to Arthur, 20% will be withheld. Arthur could then make a rollover within 60 days to an IRA or another employer plan, but an amount equal to the withheld portion must be included in the rollover or that portion will be taxable, and also be subject to the 10% penalty.

––––––––––––––––––––

Question 1.10: *How would Arthur report the lump-sum distribution in Question 1.9 if he instructs the plan administrator to make a direct rollover to an IRA, and how would he report it if he received the distribution, was subject to 20% withholding, and then completed a rollover himself within the 60-day rollover period?*

Answer: A direct rollover of the $100,000 lump sum to an IRA or another employer plan will be reported to Arthur and the IRS on Form 1099-R, although the transfer is not taxable. On Form 1099-R, $100,000 will be shown as the gross distribution, and distribution code G will be used. There would not be any withholding. On his tax return, Arthur would report $100,000 on the line for total pensions and annuities, and then enter zero on the line for the taxable amount.

If Arthur received the distribution himself, 20% withholding will apply. The plan will pay him $80,000 and withhold a tax of $20,000. If Arthur rolls over $100,000 to an IRA within 60 days, the entire rollover is tax free. He would then report $100,000 on the line for total pensions and annuities and zero as the taxable amount. However, if Arthur rolled over less than $100,000 within the 60-day period, the amount not rolled over would be reported on his tax return as the taxable amount. He will receive a federal withholding tax credit of $20,000.

Note on withholding: The 20% withholding rule does not apply to IRAs. It only applies to distributions from qualified employer plans that are eligible for rollover. IRA distributions payable on demand are subject to withholding at a flat 10% rate, but you can elect to completely avoid withholding on Form W-4P.

The Separation from Service Exception to the Penalty:

For employees who retire or leave their job after reaching age 55, a special exception to the 10% early distribution penalty applies, as discussed in the next series of questions.

Question 1.11: *What does "separation from service" mean?*

Answer: The term separation from service includes all reasons for ending the employment relationship. For example, you have separated from service if you have retired, left a company for another job, are disabled, or were fired.

Question 1.12: *Ralph Peters is age 55 in 1997. He is a participant in the XYZ Corporation Profit Sharing Plan. Pursuant to the provisions of the plan, Ralph receives a within service distribution of $10,000 in 1997 from the profit-sharing plan. Ralph has not separated from service with the employer. Ralph does not roll over the distribution into an IRA. Is Ralph subject to the 10% early distribution penalty on this $10,000 distribution?*

Answer: Yes. The 10% early distribution penalty applies since Ralph did not separate from service with the employer. The penalty of $1,000 (10% of $10,000) is in addition to the regular income tax on the $10,000 distribution.

Question 1.13: *If Ralph had retired, would he avoid the early distribution penalty?*

Answer: If Ralph retired after attaining age 55 and then requested the distribution of $10,000, the 10% early distribution penalty would not apply.

Question 1.14: *Will the XYZ Corporation Profit Sharing Plan withhold taxes from Ralph's distribution?*

Answer: Yes. Under the law, the plan administrator or plan trustee must withhold $2,000, 20% of the plan distribution of $10,000.

The withholding requirement applies whether or not Ralph is separated from service.

Question 1.15: *How can Ralph avoid the 20% withholding of $2,000 described in your answer to Question 1.14?*

Answer: Ralph may request the plan trustee to make the $10,000 check payable to Ralph's IRA. This is called a "direct rollover." On a direct rollover, the 20% withholding requirement is eliminated.

Question 1.16: *If Ralph separates from service at age 55 and arranges a direct rollover to an IRA as suggested in Question 1.15, can he withdraw the $10,000 check from the IRA without being subject to the 10% early distribution penalty?*

Answer: Not before age 59 ½. The age 55 separation-from-service exception is not applicable to distributions from an IRA. Once the funds are received in Ralph's IRA, then the IRA distribution rules are triggered. Unfortunately, distributions from an IRA after age 55 and prior to age 59 ^{1}/$_2$ are subject to the 10% early distribution penalty, although a distribution from the employer's plan after age 55 would qualify for the separation-from-service exception.

Question 1.17: *What should Ralph do if he needs the distribution from the profit-sharing plan in 1997 and does not wish to pay the 10% early distribution penalty?*

Answer: Ralph must request a $10,000 distribution (see Question 1.14) which will be subject to the 20% withholding tax of $2,000. He will avoid the 10% early distribution penalty since he is age 55 and has separated from service with his employer. Ralph will receive a net check of $8,000 from the plan but he will report on his income tax return for the calendar year 1997 $10,000 as a plan distribution and receive a federal withholding tax credit of $2,000.

Question 1.18: *Jack Marshall works for ABC University and is a participant in a 403(b) annuity contract. If he separates from service at age 56, may he receive distributions from the annuity contract without being subject to the 10% early distribution penalty?*

Answer: Yes. A 403(b) annuity contract is a qualified retirement plan subject to the 10% penalty rules and the penalty exceptions. If Jack separates from service after reaching age 55, then the distributions from the annuity contract are not subject to the 10% early distribution penalty.

Question 1.19: *Melanie Miller, at age 56, separates from service with her employer in 1997. Can she tap her IRA in 1997 without being subject to the 10% early distribution penalty?*

Answer: No. The separation-from-service rule does not apply to distributions that are made to Melanie from her IRA. The fact that she separated from service with her employer has no bearing on the tax treatment of distributions from her IRA. Distributions received by Melanie from her employer plan would not be subject to the 10% penalty based on the age 55 separation-from-service exception.

Question 1.20: *How would Melanie be taxed if she received a $16,000 net distribution from her employer's plan after separating from service and in the same year she withdrew $15,000 from her IRA?*

Answer: Assuming Melanie does not rollover any part of the $16,000 net distribution, she would have to report as income on her federal tax return a taxable distribution of $20,000, the amount of the lump sum prior to withholding. Melanie received the net check of $16,000 after the distribution of $20,000 was reduced by a 20% withholding of $4,000. The $20,000 distribution from the qualified plan is not subject to the 10% early distribution penalty under the separation-from-service exception.

The $15,000 distribution from the IRA is taxable and also is subject to a 10% early distribution penalty of $1,500 since the separation-from-service exception does not apply to IRA distributions.

The Disability Exception to the Penalty:

The disability exception applies to distributions from IRAs as well as from qualified employer retirement plans.

Question 1.21: *James Allen maintains an IRA that has an account balance of $50,000. He becomes permanently disabled in 1998, at age 54. James needs funds and would like to take $10,000 from his IRA in 1998. May he receive $10,000 from his IRA in 1998 and not be subject to the 10% early distribution penalty?*

Answer: Yes. One of the exceptions to the 10% early distribution penalty is for a distribution that is made as a result of being permanently disabled within the meaning of the Internal Revenue Code. The distributions are, however, subject to regular income tax.

Question 1.22: *What is the definition of disabled under the law?*

Answer: Under the Internal Revenue Code an individual is considered disabled "if he or she is unable to engage in any substantial gainful activity by reason of any medically determinable physical or mental impairment which can be expected to result in death or to be of long-continued and indefinite duration. An individual shall not be considered to be disabled unless he furnishes proof of the existence thereof in such form and manner as the Secretary may require."

Question 1.23: *Assume that Martin Jones is receiving Social Security disability benefits. Can Martin withdraw distributions from his IRA at age 54 without being subject to the 10% early distribution penalty?*

Answer: Maybe, if he meets the Internal Revenue Code definition of disability. According to the IRS and the United States Tax Court, Martin must provide medical evidence that his physical condition precludes him from engaging in substantial gainful activity and can be expected to result in death or to be of long-continued or indefinite duration. This definition is not the same as the requirement for receiving Social Security disability benefits.

Question 1.24: *Fran Davis is age 52 and employed by the ABC Corporation. The ABC Corporation maintains a defined benefit pension plan. Fran becomes permanently disabled at age 52 and is entitled to a pension of $100 per month. Is Fran subject to the 10% early distribution penalty on her pension?*

Answer: No. A distribution to Fran before she reaches age 59 ½ from the ABC Corporation's defined benefit plan on the basis of her permanent disability is exempt from the 10% early distribution penalty.

Question 1.25: *A taxpayer, age 50, is under medical treatment for a physical or mental illness. Until the treatment is completed, his ability to earn a living is diminished. Are current distributions from his IRA automatically exempt from the 10% early distribution penalty?*

Answer: No. According to the United States Tax Court and the IRS regulations, the impairment must be expected to last for an indefinite period and must be irremediable. An impairment that is remediable is not a disability under the tax law. According to the IRS regulations an individual is not considered disabled if with reasonable effort the impairment can be diminished to the extent that the individual will not be prevented by the impairment from engaging in his customary or any comparable substantial gainful activity.

Question 1.26: *Al Bryant is age 54 and permanently disabled. His IRA account in 1997 amounts to $50,000. He would like to withdraw distributions from his IRA from time to time over the next few years as he needs funds. May he withdraw funds from his IRA at random without being subject to the 10% early distribution penalty?*

Answer: Yes. According to the IRS in Letter Ruling 9318043, dated February 11, 1993, a disabled taxpayer may withdraw funds from the IRA in unequal, non periodic payments and will not be subject to the 10% early distribution penalty.

The Substantially Equal Payment Exception to the 10% Early Distribution Penalty:

Distributions taken from an employer plan after separation from service as part of a series of substantially equal payments are not subject to an early distribution penalty, regardless of your age. Similarly, there is no penalty on IRA withdrawals that qualify under the substantially equal payments test.

Question 1.27: *How does an employee satisfy the substantially equal payment test?*

Answer: The law requires that distributions to a former employee who has separated from service be "part of a series of substantially equal periodic payments (not less frequently than annually) made for the life (or life expectancy) of the employee or the joint lives (or joint life expectancies) of such employee and his or her designated beneficiary." The age of the employee does not matter.

Question 1.28: *Has the IRS established any ground rules on how the substantially equal payment test applies?*

Answer: Yes. IRS issued Notice 89-25 dated March 20, 1989 on how to apply the substantially equal payment test. The IRS permits the substantially equal payment rule to be satisfied under one of the following three methods:

a. Method 1 - Uses a life expectancy approach. This method divides the account balance by the applicable life expectancy, which is found in IRS tables (see Question 1.34). This is the same life expectancy approach used under the IRS' minimum required distribution rules for those over age 70 ¹/₂, discussed in Chapter 2.

b. Method 2 - Uses an amortization approach. This method computes equal payments using the same life expectancy as under Method 1 and a reasonable rate of interest.

c. Method 3 - Uses an annuity approach. This method computes payments using the annuity factor from the UP 1984 mortality table and a reasonable rate of interest.

Question 1.29: *Does the substantially equal payment rule apply to distributions from an IRA?*

Answer: Yes. IRS Publication 590 (1994 version) states as follows:

> You can receive distributions from your IRA that are part of a series of substantially equal payments over your life (or your life expectancy) or over the lives of you and your beneficiary (or your joint life expectancies) without having to pay the 10% additional tax, even if you receive such distributions before you are age 59 ¹/₂. You must use an IRS approved distribution method and must take at least one distribution annually for this exception to apply.

Question 1.30: *If you wish to tap your IRA before age 59 ¹/₂ under the substantially equal payment rule, must you separate from service with your employer?*

Answer: No. The law does not require that you, as an IRA owner, separate from service with your employer in order to use the substantially equal payment rule.

Question 1.31: *Which of the three methods should an IRA owner under age 59 ¹/₂ use in order to satisfy the substantially equal payment rule?*

Answer: The amortization method (Method 2) is probably the easiest to work with. It is similar to the fixed payments that one makes on his or her home mortgage. The factors that go into the computation of the annual payments are principal, interest rate, and period of time.

Question 1.32: *Can you illustrate how the amortization method works?*

Answer: The IRS in Notice 89-25, dated March 20, 1989, illustrates the amortization method and states the following:

> "Payments...will be treated as substantially equal periodic payments...if the amount to be distributed annually is determined by amortizing the taxpayer's account balance over a number of years equal to the life expectancy of the account owner or the joint life and last survivor expectancy of the account owner and beneficiary (with life expectancies determined in accordance with proposed section 1.401(a)(9)-1 of the regulations) at an interest rate that does not exceed a reasonable interest rate on the date payment commences. For example, a 50-year-old individual with a life expectancy of 33.1, having an account balance of $100,000, and assuming an interest rate of 8 percent, could satisfy (the substantially equal payment rule) ...by distributing $8,679 annually, deemed by amortizing $100,000 over 33.1 years at 8% interest."

Question 1.33: *Does the IRA owner using the amortization method described above have a choice of using a single life expectancy table or a joint life expectancy table?*

Answer: Yes. IRS Notice 89-25 permits the IRA owner to select which life expectancy table to use.

Question 1.34: *Where are the IRS life expectancy tables found?*

Answer: The IRS regulations have tables that are based upon a single life expectancy or a joint life expectancy. These tables are reproduced in the Appendix. The tables are from section 1.72-9 of the IRS regulations. Table V of the regulations is used for a single life expectancy and Table VI of the regulations is used for a joint life expectancy. IRS Publication 590 refers to Table V of the regulations as Table I, and Table VI of the regulations as Table II. In the Appendix of this book are Tables I and II from Publication 590.

Question 1.35: *What interest rate is used under the amortization method?*

Answer: According to the IRS an interest rate that does not exceed a reasonable rate of interest on the date payment commenced should be used. The IRA owner could, for example, use 120 percent of the long-term applicable federal rate. Alternatively, he or she may ask a local bank what the fixed rate is for a long-term mortgage and use that rate. The IRS has been flexible in terms of rates that may be used by IRA owners.

Question 1.36: *How do the life expectancy tables work?*

Answer: According to IRS, if a single life expectancy is used, then the life expectancy of the IRA owner is based upon the IRA owner's attained age as of his or her birthday in the calendar year in which distributions commence. If a joint life expectancy is used, then the life expectancy of the IRA owner and his or her beneficiary would be based upon their attained ages as of their birthdays in the calendar year in which distributions commence.

For example, if Jack Adams, an IRA owner, is age 49 on his birthday in 1997, has no beneficiary and commences IRA distributions in 1997 under the amortization method, then he must use a 34-year single life expectancy for purposes of determining the amount of the annual payments. If you check IRS Table I in the Appendix, you will see that 34 years is the life expectancy of a 49-year-old person; the table is used by men and women.

If Jack has designated his wife, Mary, age 48 in 1997, as his beneficiary and commences distributions, then he may use a joint life expectancy of 40.7 years for purposes of determining the amount of the annual payments. The joint life expectancy of 40.7 years is shown in IRS Table II in the Appendix, in the column where ages 49 and 48 intersect.

Question 1.37: *Assume that Jack is eligible to use either a single life expectancy or joint life expectancy in 1997 in order to calculate the annual payments. He uses a single life expectancy table in 1997. May Jack switch to the joint life expectancy table in 1998?*

Answer: No. Under the amortization method, once the amount of the annual payments has been established, it cannot be changed. It is similar to payments on a fixed-rate mortgage, which becomes fixed for the duration of the mortgage.

Question 1.38: *If the amortization method is selected, may the IRA owner receive monthly or quarterly payments?*

Answer: Yes. However, a reasonable interest rate (see Question 1.35) must be used to reflect the frequency of payments.

Question 1.39: *Assume that Marvin Bardiner is age 52 in 1998 and has four separate IRAs in his name. He would like to currently tap only one of his IRAs and take advantage of the substantially equal payment rule. May he receive distributions from only one IRA and satisfy the substantially equal payment rule?*

Answer: Yes. The IRS has issued several letter rulings that indicate that each IRA stands on its own and that the law does not require that IRAs be aggregated in order to calculate a series of substantially equal payments (see Question 1.27).

Question 1.40: *If Marvin uses the amortization method (see Method 2 under Question 1.28) in calculating his substantially equal payments from IRA No. 1, must he use the same method if he decides to tap IRA No. 2 prior to age 59 1/2?*

Answer: No. Each IRA stands on its own. If Marvin decides to tap another of his IRAs before age 59 1/2, any one of the three methods discussed in Question 1.28 can be used with respect to distributions from that IRA. The fact that Marvin tapped IRA No. 1 prior to age 59 1/2 does not mean he must tap any other IRA prior to age 59 1/2.

Question 1.41: *Assume that Marvin, age 52, uses the amortization method and a single life expectancy of 31.3 years in calculating his annual payments from IRA No. 1. If Marvin commences distributions from IRA No. 1 at age 52 under the substantially equal payment rule, must he continue to receive payments over a 31.3-year period?*

Answer: No. IRS Publication 590 states that the substantially equal payments must continue for at least five years or until an individual reaches age 59 1/2, whichever is the longer period. Since Marvin commenced his substantially equal payments at age 52, he must continue to receive such payments until he attains age 59 1/2.

Question 1.42: *What happens if Marvin in 2004 at age 58 voluntarily decides to discontinue receiving his payments from IRA No. 1?*

Answer: As discussed in Question 1.41, payments must continue under the substantially equal payments test for a minimum of five years or until you are age 59 1/2, whichever is the longer period. Here, the longer period ends when Marvin attains age 59 1/2. The act of discontinuing the payments before the end of this minimum period is deemed to be a modification of the amortization method and triggers the 10% early distribution penalty. According to the law, Marvin's tax for the year 2004, the year in which the modification takes place, is increased by the amount of the 10% early distribution penalty that would have been paid on the early distributions if the substantially equal payment rule was not applicable.

Question 1.43: *How much would Marvin's penalty be under the facts of Question 1.42?*

Answer: Assume that Marvin was required to receive $10,000 per year from IRA No. 1 under the amortization method (Method 2 under Question 1.28). He would have received the following amounts:

Marvin's Age	Year	Amount received from IRA No. 1
52	1998	$ 10,000
53	1999	10,000
54	2000	10,000
55	2001	10,000
56	2002	10,000
57	2003	10,000
58	2004	-0-
		$ 60,000

Since Marvin voluntarily discontinues the receipt of annual payments from IRA No. 1 in 2004, he must pay an additional 10% early distribution penalty to the IRS with his income tax return for 2004. The penalty is $6,000, which is equal to 10% of all the amounts received by Martin before age 59 ¹/₂. In addition, he must pay interest on the $6,000 early distribution penalty on a retroactive basis.

Question 1.44: *If Marvin died at age 58 in the calendar year 2004, would the $6,000 early distribution penalty described in your answer to Question 1.43 be applicable?*

Answer: No. The law states that if the substantially equal payments are subsequently modified as a result of death, then the additional early distribution penalty is not applicable.

Question 1.45: *If Marvin becomes permanently disabled at age 58 in the calendar year 2004, would the $6,000 early distribution penalty described in your answer to Question 1.43 be applicable?*

Answer: No. The law states that if the substantially equal payments are subsequently modified as a result of disability, then the additional tax is not applicable.

Question 1.46: *If Marvin became temporarily disabled at age 58 in the calendar year 2004, would the $6,000 additional tax described in your answer to Question 1.43 be applicable?*

Answer: The law does not define the word "disability" in the context of a subsequent modification of the substantially equal payment rule but it is obvious that a permanent type of disability would be necessary in order to avoid the $6,000 additional tax.

Question 1.47: *Assume that Marvin's brother Gregory is age 56 in 1998 when he decides to tap his IRA on a monthly basis starting on July 1, 1998. He uses the amortization method (see Method 2 under Question 1.28) until he attains age 59 ¹/₂ in 2001 and then voluntarily stops receiving distributions from his IRA. Has Gregory's voluntary act in 2001 triggered an early distribution penalty?*

Answer: Yes. Gregory's act of voluntarily ceasing distributions from his IRA in 2001 constitutes a modification of the amortization method. Since the modification takes place before the close of the five-year period beginning with the date of the first payment, Gregory is subject to the early distribution penalty on all distributions he received prior to age 59 ¹/₂. The voluntary modification in this case should not have taken place prior to July 1, 2003 since the close of the five-year period is June 30, 2003.

Question 1.48: *If an IRA owner age 50 dies and the death benefits from the IRA are paid to his estate, will the estate be subject to the 10% early distribution penalty?*

Answer: No. IRA death benefits payable to an estate are exempt from the 10% early distribution penalty.

Question 1.49: *If Craig, an IRA owner age 60, dies and has the death benefits of his IRA payable to his son Joseph, age 30, will Joseph be subject to the 10% early distribution penalty?*

Answer: No. IRA death benefits that are payable to a designated beneficiary are exempt from the 10% early distribution penalty. The age of the beneficiary is not important. The law states that the 10% early distribution penalty is not applicable to death benefits that are paid to a beneficiary.

Question 1.50: *Assume that in Question 1.49, Craig died at age 58. Will his son, Joseph, be subject to the 10% early distribution penalty?*

Answer: No. The fact that the IRA owner was under age 59¹/₂ at the time of his death does not change the rule that the beneficiary is not subject to the 10% early distribution penalty.

CHAPTER 2

You Must Begin Minimum
Distributions at Age 70½

The longer you can keep funds in your IRA or employer plan without withdrawing them, the more money you can accumulate tax-free for your retirement years and, ultimately, for your heirs. However, the tax law does not allow you to delay the start of distribution indefinitely.

When you reach age 70½, you must begin to receive minimum annual distributions from your plan. The IRS has established a series of complex rules for determining the minimum amount you must receive each year. Penalties can be imposed by the IRS if the rules are not followed. The distribution methods are the same for IRAs as for qualified employer plans. However, proposed legislation being considered by Congress when this book went to press would delay the qualified employer plan beginning date for employees (except 5% owners) who continue to work beyond the age in which they reach age 70½; see the answer to Question 2.3.

In general, the minimum amount that you must withdraw each year is based upon your life expectancy and the life expectancy of you and your beneficiary. Your choice of beneficiary and distribution method will affect not only your minimum required distribution, but also the amounts that your beneficiaries will have to receive, and pay tax on, after your death. This chapter will introduce you to the minimum distribution requirements. Subsequent chapters will highlight the specific rules that apply when your designated beneficiary is your spouse (Chapter 3); a child, grandchild, or other beneficiary who is more than 10 years younger than you are (Chapter 4); or other adult beneficiary (Chapter 6).

The focus throughout this book is on meeting the minimum distribution requirements, but if you have substantial retirement plan holdings, you and your professional advisor should consider planning steps to avoid the 15% excess distribution penalty, mentioned on page 1.

Minimum Distribution Basics:

The following series of questions and answers illustrate the application of the required minimum distribution rules.

Question 2.1: *What type of retirement accounts are subject to the required minimum distribution rules?*

Answer: Distributions from qualified plans such as 401(k) plans or profit-sharing plans, qualified annuity plans, individual retirement accounts, individual retirement annuities, 403(b) annuity contacts, and certain deferred compensation plans of state and local governments and tax exempt organizations are subject to the required minimum distribution rules.

Question 2.2: *What is the required beginning date for minimum distributions?*

Answer: Generally, the required beginning date is April 1 of the calendar year following the calendar year in which the plan participant reaches age 70^1/$_2$.

Question 2.3: *Are there any exceptions to the rule that the required beginning date is April 1 of the calendar year following the calendar year in which an individual attains age 70^1/$_2$?*

Answer: Yes. There are several technical exceptions to the general definition of required beginning date.

If you are an employee who attained age 70^1/$_2$ before January 1, 1988, and you are not a 5% owner of the business, then your required beginning date is April 1 of the calendar year following the calendar year in which you retire, even though that date is later than April 1 of the calendar year following the calendar year in which you attain age 70^1/$_2$.

Similarily, if you are a participant in a qualified plan that is a government plan or church plan, the required beginning date is April 1 of the calendar year following the calendar year in which you retire, even though that date is later than April 1 of the calendar year following the calendar year in which you attain age 70^1/$_2$.

Under proposed legislation being considered when this book went to press, the same exception would be extended to all employees who continue to work beyond the year in which they reach age 70^1/$_2$, provided they are not 5% owners. In other words, for employees other than 5% owners, the required beginning date for distribution from the employee's plan would be April 1 of the calendar year following the later of (1) the calendar year in which the employee attains age 70^1/$_2$, or (2) the calendar year in which the employee retires. Check with the administrator of your employer's plan or your professional advisor for the status of this proposed legislation. The proposal would not affect the required beginning date for IRA distributions.

Another example involves 403(b) annuity contracts. The IRS stated in Letter Ruling 9345044, dated August 16, 1993, that the pre-1987 account-balance in a 403(b) annuity contract may be subject to a special rule. If the issuer or custodian of a section 403(b) contract maintains records that enable it to identify the value of the account balance under the section 403(b) account as of December 31, 1986, then distributions of that pre-1987 balance do not have to begin until the employee or retired employee attains age 75.

Question 2.4: *When is an employee considered to be a 5% owner of a business?*

Answer: An employee is considered to be a 5% owner if at any time on or after age 66^1/$_2$ the employee owns directly or indirectly more than 5% of the stock of the corporation or if the employer is not a corporation, the plan participant owns directly or indirectly more than 5% of the capital or profit interest in the employer.

Question 2.5: *On June 1, 1997 Martin Mitchell will attain age 64. He has an IRA that has in excess of $100,000 and would like to withdraw approximately $20,000 from it for three years. May Martin do so without being subject to any IRS penalties?*

Answer: Yes. All he should be concerned about is paying taxes on the distributions from his IRA. Since he has attained age 59¹/₂, he is not subject to the 10% early distribution penalty described in the previous chapter.

Question 2.6: *Once Martin takes the $20,000 distribution from his IRA at age 64, must he continue to do so for each year after reaching age 64?*

Answer: No. Since Martin has not attained his required beginning date, he is free to take distributions from his IRA at age 64 or in later years before the required beginning date without regard to the minimum distribution rules. He does not have to take any further distributions if he does not want to, until he reaches his required beginning date.

Question 2.7: *When does Martin reach his required beginning date?*

Answer: Based upon existing law, Martin's required beginning date is April 1 following the calendar year in which he attains age 70¹/₂. Assume Martin is age 64 on June 1, 1997. He is therefore age 70 on June 1, 2003 and age 70¹/₂ on December 1, 2003. Martin's required beginning date is April 1, 2004.

Question 2.8: *If Martin dies prior to his required beginning date of April 1, 2004, what distribution rules are applicable to his IRA beneficiary?*

Answer: Specific death benefit distribution rules are applicable. Those rules depend upon who the beneficiary is and whether or not the five-year rule or the exception to the five-year rule applies. It also depends on whether or not a surviving spouse is involved, since a surviving spouse is eligible to create a spousal rollover IRA account. These rules are discussed in detail throughout this book.

Question 2.9: *If Martin is alive on his required beginning date of April 1, 2004, how will he determine the amount that he must receive as a required minimum distribution from his IRA?*

Answer: The following information is necessary in order to determine the amount that Martin must receive as a required minimum distribution from his IRA:

a. The distribution calendar year that is involved in the computation.

b. The IRA account balance as of the valuation date.

c. His age.

d. The age of his designated beneficiary.

e. Whether the designated beneficiary was timely selected.

f. Whether the recalculation method is applicable.

g. Whether the term-certain method is applicable.

h. Whether the hybrid method is applicable.

i. Whether the Minimum Distribution Incidental Benefit Requirement (MDIB Requirement) is applicable.

The terms used in (a)–(i) are explained in the following questions and answers.

Question 2.10: *What is meant by the term "distribution calendar year"?*

Answer: A distribution calendar year is a calendar year with respect to which a taxpayer must receive a required minimum distribution.

Question 2.11: *What does the term "first distribution calendar year" mean?*

Answer: The first calendar year for which a distribution is required is called the first distribution calendar year.

Question 2.12: *What is Martin's first distribution calendar year?*

Answer: Martin's required beginning date is April 1, 2004, but his first distribution calendar year is 2003. The year 2003 is the calendar year in which Martin attains age $70^1/_2$.

Question 2.13: *Must Martin receive his required minimum distribution for the calendar year 2003 in 2003?*

Answer: No. Martin may receive his required minimum distribution for the calendar year 2003 by no later than April 1, 2004, the required beginning date. The IRS rules permit a distribution for the individual's first distribution calendar year to be made by no later than his required beginning date.

Question 2.14: *May Martin receive his required minimum distribution for the first distribution calendar year 2003 in 2003?*

Answer: Yes. Martin may receive his required minimum distribution for the first distribution calendar year 2003 in 2003.

Question 2.15: *May Martin receive his required minimum distribution for the first distribution calendar year 2003 partially in 2003 and partially in 2004?*

Answer: Yes. He can allocate his required minimum distribution for his first distribution calendar year 2003 in any manner he wishes provided that it is completely paid by no later than his required beginning date of April 1, 2004. Thus, Martin may receive his required minimum distribution for his first distribution calendar year 2003 between the period commencing January 1, 2003 and ending April 1, 2004. Distributions will be taxable in the year Martin receives them.

Question 2.16: *Must Martin receive his required minimum distribution for his second distribution calendar year 2004 in 2004?*

Answer: Yes. The required minimum distribution for all subsequent distribution calendar years after the first distribution calendar year must be received by no later than December 31 of that distribution year. Thus, required minimum distributions for his second distribution calendar year and years thereafter must be received on or before December 31 of such distribution calendar year.

Life Expectancy Methods:

The following questions and answers illustrate how your choice of life expectancy method affects the minimum distributions you must receive.

Question 2.17: *Assume that Martin is single. Over what period of time may Martin receive required minimum distributions from his IRA?*

Answer: Martin may receive his required minimum distributions from his IRA over a period that does not exceed his single life expectancy, or over a period that does not exceed the joint life expectancy of Martin and his designated beneficiary.

Question 2.18: *How is Martin's single life expectancy determined?*

Answer: From IRS life expectancy tables. In the Appendix, we include the single life expectancy table found in IRS Publication 590, which the IRS refers to as Table I. In section 1.72–9 of the Income Tax Regulations, this same table is included, but it is labeled as Table V.

Question 2.19: *What age does Martin use when applying the IRS life expectancy table?*

Answer: Martin's life expectancy is based upon his attained age as of his birthday in his "first distribution calendar year" (Question 2.12), the calendar year he attains age $70^1/_2$.

Assume Martin will be age 70 on June 1, 2003 and age $70^1/_2$ on December 1, 2003. In the calendar year 2003, Martin's attained age is age 70. Therefore, age 70 is Martin's attained age for purposes of looking up his life expectancy in the IRS table.

As shown in the Appendix, IRS Table I from Publication 590 provides that a single individual age 70 has a 16-year life expectancy.

Question 2.20: *If Martin uses a single life expectancy table, must he receive required minimum distributions from his IRA for his life expectancy of 16 years?*

Answer: No. The law allows Martin to accelerate the distributions from his IRA from time to time, so all withdrawals may be completed before 16 years.

Question 2.21: *If Martin wants to use the joint life expectancy method instead of the single life expectancy method, and his beneficiary is his sister Sara, who will be age 64 on her birthday in 2003, how would he determine their joint life expectancy?*

Answer: Joint life expectancy is determined under IRS Table II from IRS Publication 590, which is shown in the Appendix. In section 1.72–9 of the Income Tax Regulations, this same table is included, but it is labeled as Table VI.

Using their attained ages of 70 and 64 in 2003, Martin's first distribution calendar year, Table II in the Appendix shows that Martin and Sara have a joint life expectancy of 23.7 years.

Question 2.22: *Martin has been told that he may receive distributions from his IRA based upon his single life expectancy or joint life expectancy under one of two methods. What are the two methods that may be used in calculating his required minimum distributions from his IRA?*

Answer: The law generally permits Martin to receive his required minimum distributions from his IRA under either the term-certain method or the recalculation method.

Under the term-certain method, the initial single or joint life expectancy used by Martin would be reduced by one in each subsequent year. Under the recalculation method, Martin's initial life expectancy would be refigured for each year based upon his attained age in that year. The life expectancy of a spousal beneficiary may also be recalculated, but the life expectancy of a nonspouse beneficiary may not be recalculated. A nonspousal beneficiary is required to use the term-certain method.

Examples of both methods are provided later in this chapter and throughout this book.

Question 2.23: *Is it more advantageous to use the term-certain method or the recalculation method?*

Answer: In general terms, the recalculation method allows you to take smaller required minimum distributions. This is because life expectancy is reduced each year by less than one under the recalculation method, while under the term-certain method life expectancy is reduced by a full year.

However, where minimum distributions are based on joint life expectancy, the term-certain method, besides being easier to apply, is generally more advantageous to the beneficiary following the IRA owner's death. This is because under the term-certain method, the beneficiary may spread out distributions over the balance of the initial term-certain joint life expectancy. Under the recalculation method, the life expectancy of a recalculating owner is reduced to zero in the year following the year of the owner's death. As a result, distributions to the beneficiary must then be based solely on the beneficiary's remaining life expectancy. Similarly, if the beneficiary were the owner's spouse whose life expectancy was being recalculated, and the spouse died first, the owner's single life expectancy would have to be used to determine the required minimum distributions for years following the year of the spouse's death.

Examples comparing the two distribution methods are provided throughout this book.

Question 2.24: *Assuming the owner of an IRA would like to elect the term-certain method of distribution, is that method always available?*

Answer: No. The IRA plan document must be consulted in order to determine whether or not the term certain method is available. A number of financial institutions have distribution forms that permit the IRA owner to elect the term-certain method or the recalculation method. However, many financial institutions do not have election forms. If the financial institution permits the term-certain method to be elected but does not have an election form, then the IRA owner must create his or her own election form. The election must be made by no later than the IRA owner's required beginning date.

Question 2.25: *Do some financial institutions use words other than "term certain" that are the equivalents of the meaning of the words "term certain"?*

Answer: Yes. Some institutions may use such terms as:

   a.   fixed period

   b.   fixed period of time

   c.   nonrecalculation method

   d.   once computed

   e.   election out of the recalculation method

f. election not to refigure life expectancy

g. declining-balance

Question 2.26: *What does the IRS say about whether or not an IRA owner may elect the term-certain method?*

Answer: The IRS states that the IRA plan document must be examined in order to determine whether or not you may elect to use the term-certain method. The IRS does not use the words "term-certain" but uses equivalent language such as "election not to recalculate life expectancy."

Question 2.27: *Assume that a term-certain method is available under the terms of the IRA plan document. What does the IRS say about the mechanics of making the term-certain election?*

Answer: Unfortunately, the IRS guidelines on how the election is to be made are general in nature. The IRS states that the election must be made by the IRA owner by no later than the IRA owner's required beginning date. In addition, according to the IRS the election is irrevocable as of the IRA owner's required beginning date.

Question 2.28: *Assume that the IRA owner wishes to make the term-certain election with respect to his or her IRA. What action should be taken in order to protect the IRA owner against an IRS challenge at a later date?*

Answer: The IRA owner should make a written election with the IRA institution by no later than his or her required beginning date. The written election should be sent to the appropriate responsible person at the IRA institution by certified mail, return receipt requested. In order to avoid a technical problem, the election should be sent to the IRA institution well in advance of the required beginning date so that it is received by the IRA institution by no later than the required beginning date. A copy of the letter and written election should be retained in a permanent file. The written election should indicate such information as the following:

1. The name of the IRA owner.

2. The name of the IRA financial institution.

3. The account number of the IRA.

4. That the term-certain method is being elected in calculating his or her required minimum distributions.

5. The period of the term-certain that is to be used in order to calculate the required minimum distributions.

6. A statement by the IRA owner that his or her life expectancy shall not be recalculated and that the spouse's life expectancy shall not be recalculated if the spouse is the designated beneficiary.

7. A statement that the term-certain method shall be irrevocable and binding for the first distribution calendar year and all subsequent years.

8. The signature of the IRA owner and the date he or she signed the election.

Question 2.29: *Assume that the IRA institution plan document permits the term-certain election. Further assume that the financial institution has its own election form that contains some basic information such as the name of the IRA owner, the name of the IRA financial institution, and the account number of the IRA account. The form further states that the IRA owner may check either a box that states that the term-certain method is applicable or another box that states that the recalculation method is applicable. The form must be signed and dated by the IRA owner. Assume that the IRA owner fills out the form properly, signs and dates it, checks the term-certain box, and sends it back to the IRA institution by no later than his or her required beginning date. Has the IRA owner made a valid written election of the term-certain method?*

Answer: Probably. The IRS does not indicate how the election should be made or upon whom the election should be served. In the absence of any court decision, regulation, or ruling to the contrary, the above action by the IRA owner should be sufficient to demonstrate that a term-certain election has been made. The IRS is interested in the IRA owner's timely decision to make an election. The actions by the IRA owner are clear evidence of his or her intention to make a term-certain election. The IRS would have to permit the maximum term period to be used in this situation, since the IRS has not issued any guidelines on what should be contained in the election or the mechanics of making the election.

Question 2.30: *Assume Martin elects the term-certain method and his single life expectancy of 16 years. His estate is the beneficiary of the IRA. Can you show what life expectancy he would use to figure his required minimum distribution each year?*

Answer: The following schedule reflects the application of the term-certain method.

Age	Distribution year	Calendar year	Remaining Term-Certain Period
70	1	2003	16
71	2	2004	15
72	3	2005	14
73	4	2006	13
74	5	2007	12
75	6	2008	11
76	7	2009	10
77	8	2010	9
78	9	2011	8
79	10	2012	7
80	11	2013	6
81	12	2014	5
82	13	2015	4
83	14	2016	3
84	15	2017	2
85	16	2018	1
86	17	2019	0

Question 2.31: *Assume that Martin's IRA account balance as of December 31, 2002 is $96,000. How much is Martin's required minimum distribution that is attributable to his first distribution calendar year 2003?*

Answer: $6,000. Martin's first distribution calendar year is 2003. The year 2003 is the year he attained age 70$\frac{1}{2}$. In order to determine his required minimum distribution for the first distribution calendar year 2003, he must use the value of his IRA account balance as of the end of the prior year, which is then divided by the appropriate life expectancy that is applicable to the first distribution calendar year 2003. The account balance as of December 31, 2002 of $96,000 is divided by 16 years, which is the life expectancy of Martin in the first distribution calendar year 2003. The result is $6,000.

Question 2.32: *Must Martin receive the required minimum distribution of $6,000 that is attributable to his first distribution calendar year 2003 by December 31, 2003?*

Answer: No. The law states that he may receive his required minimum distribution for his first distribution calendar year of 2003 by no later than his required beginning date, which is April 1, 2004. His required beginning date, as you may recall, is April 1 of the calendar year following the calendar year in which he attained age 70$\frac{1}{2}$. He attained age 70$\frac{1}{2}$ in 2003.

Question 2.33: *Assume that Martin received his $6,000 required minimum distribution for his first distribution calendar year 2003 on October 31, 2003. Further assume that his account balance in his IRA as of December 31, 2003 is $96,700, taking into account earnings during 2003 and the $6000 distribution. How much must Martin receive during the second distribution calendar year 2004 under the term-certain method in order to satisfy the required minimum distribution rules for the year 2004?*

Answer: $6,446.67. The calendar year 2004 is Martin's second distribution calendar year. He must receive his required minimum distribution for his second distribution calendar year by December 31, 2004.

In order to determine his required minimum distribution for the calendar year 2004, the value of his account balance as of December 31, 2003 must be divided by the appropriate life expectancy that is applicable to the calendar year 2004. The account balance of $96,700 is divided by 15 years, which is Martin's remaining life expectancy under the term-certain method as of the second distribution calendar year 2004. The result is $6,446.67.

Question 2.34: *Assume that Martin received his required minimum distribution of $6,000 for his first distribution calendar year 2003 on March 31, 2004. Further assume that Martin's IRA account balance as of December 31, 2003 is $104,000. How much must Martin receive during the calendar year 2004 in order to satisfy the required minimum distributions for the second distribution calendar year 2004?*

Answer: $6,533.33. The IRS has a special rule that is only applicable if any portion of a distribution that is attributable to a first distribution calendar year is paid in the second distribution calendar year by the required beginning date. Based upon this rule, the actual balance in the IRA account as of December 31, 2003 is reduced by $6,000, since that amount is attributable to the first distribution calendar year and was paid in the second distribution calendar year on March 31, 2004, which is not later than the required beginning date of April 1, 2004.

The actual account balance of $104,000 on December 31, 2003 is hypothetically reduced by $6,000 to $98,000. The hypothetical account balance of $98,000 is divided by 15 years, which is the life expectancy of Martin as of the second distribution calendar year 2004. The result is $6,533.33, the amount Martin must receive for the second distribution calendar year 2004. It must be received by Martin by no later than December 31, 2004. Martin reports both the $6,000 distribution and the $6,533.33 distribution for a total of $12,533.33, on his Form 1040 for the calendar year 2004.

Question 2.35: *Assume the same facts as in Question 2.34 except that Martin receives a distribution of $7,000 on March 31, 2004. How much must Martin receive during the calendar year 2004 in order to satisfy the required minimum distribution rules?*

Answer: Martin must receive a total of $12,533.33 during the calendar year 2004. This is computed as follows: $7,000 was received on March 31, 2004 of which $6,000 is applicable to the first distribution calendar year 2003 and the excess of $1,000 is applied towards the required minimum distribution of $6,533.33 for the second distribution calendar year 2004. In addition, Martin must receive the balance of $5,533.33 for the second distribution calendar year 2004 by no later than December 31, 2004.

Question 2.36: *If Martin's required minimum distribution for 2003 is $6,000 and he receives a $7,000 distribution on March 31, 2004 and $5,533.33 by December 31, 2004, does he have to report the entire distribution on his Form 1040 for the calendar year 2004?*

Answer: Yes. The amount received by Martin in the calendar year 2004 must be reported by him. The fact that he receives more than his required minimum distributions in a given year makes no difference to his tax situation. Martin must report $12,533.33 in the calendar year 2004.

Question 2.37: *Assume the same facts as in Question 2.34 except that Martin receives a distribution of $17,333.33 on March 31, 2004. Is Martin entitled to a credit of $5,000 against his required minimum distribution for his third distribution calendar year 2005?*

Answer: No. If an IRA owner receives a distribution in a given distribution calendar year that exceeds the required minimum distribution for that calendar year, he or she may not receive a credit for the additional distribution against the required minimum distribution for a subsequent year. There is a limited exception for the first distribution calendar year that was previously discussed.

The $17,333.33 that Martin received on March 31, 2004 would satisfy the $6,000 required minimum distribution for the first distribution calendar year 2003 and the $6,533.33 required minimum distribution for the calendar year 2004. The fact that he received an additional distribution of $5,000, whether by accident or design, does not result in a credit towards his required minimum distribution for his third distribution calendar year 2005.

However, the entire distribution of $17,333.33 (which includes the additional $5,000 distribution) on March 31, 2004 does reduce the IRA account balance as of December 31, 2004. This has the indirect effect of reducing the amount of the required minimum distribution for the third distribution calendar year 2005 and all years thereafter.

Question 2.38: *Martin timely elected a 16-year term-certain period in which to receive his required minimum distributions from his IRA. May Martin accelerate distributions from his IRA from time to time?*

Answer: Yes. If Martin elects to receive his required minimum distributions over a 16-year term-certain period, he can accelerate distributions from his IRA from time to time. The IRS is not concerned about Martin receiving more than his required minimum distributions from his IRA.

Question 2.39: *If Martin determines that he must receive a $6,000 distribution for his first distribution calendar year of 2003, should he defer taking the distribution until the beginning of 2004?*

Answer: Martin has the option of receiving the $6,000 IRA distribution with respect to his first distribution calendar year 2003 at any time between the period January 1, 2003 and April 1, 2004. For tax purposes, he may prefer to receive the $6,000 distribution in 2004 instead of in 2003. However, if he defers the entire amount to 2004, he will have two IRA distributions to report in 2004. Martin must receive his IRA distribution for his second distribution calendar year 2004 by December 31, 2004.

Penalty for Insufficient Distributions:

The following questions and answers explain the penalty that the IRS may impose if the required minimum distribution for a year is not received.

Question 2.40: *If Martin must receive a required minimum distribution of $6,000 from his IRA for his first distribution calendar year 2003, but in December 2003, he receives only $4,000, may the IRS assess a penalty against Martin?*

Answer: No penalty will be imposed if the required $2,000 balance is received by April 1, 2004, Martin's required beginning date. If the balance is not received by April 1, 2004, the IRS may assess a penalty equal to 50% of the insufficient distribution for the first distribution year of 2003. Thus, if the remaining $2,000 were not timely received, the penalty would be $1,000.

Question 2.41: *May the IRS waive the $1,000 penalty described in the previous question?*

Answer: Yes. Martin must prove to the IRS that the shortfall was due to reasonable error and that reasonable steps are being taken to remedy the shortfall.

Question 2.42: *Assume that Martin dies on July 1, 2007, before receiving his required minimum distribution of $7,000 from his IRA for that calendar year. Is Martin's IRA beneficiary subject to an IRS penalty of $3,500 based upon the fact that Martin failed to receive his required minimum distribution of $7,000 for his fifth distribution calendar year 2007?*

Answer: No. The death of Martin prior to the end of the calendar year 2007 is obviously reasonable cause and the IRS would not assess a penalty against Martin's beneficiary. However, Martin's beneficiary should request the $7,000 required minimum distribution from Martin's IRA for the calendar year 2007 within a reasonable period of time after discovering that Martin failed to receive his required minimum distribution of $7,000 for his fifth distribution calendar year 2007.

Question 2.43: *Assume that Martin died on July 1, 2007 before receiving his required minimum distribution of $7,000 from his IRA for the fifth distribution calendar year. Martin's estate is his IRA beneficiary and the insufficient distribution is discovered by the executor of Martin's estate in 2008. Assume that the required minimum distribution that Martin would have received in 2008 had he lived would have been $7,200. What action should the executor of Martin's estate take in order to avoid any IRS penalties?*

Answer: The executor of Martin's estate should take a total distribution of $14,200 from Martin's IRA during the calendar year 2008. The executor should take the required minimum distribution of $7,000 attributable to the fifth distribution calendar year 2007 as soon as possible during 2008. The required minimum distribution of $7,200 attributable to the sixth distribution calendar year 2008 must be received by Martin's executor from Martin's IRA by no later than December 31, 2008. Such action by Martin's executor during 2008 should eliminate any IRS penalty with respect to the $7,000 shortfall for the fifth distribution calendar year 2007.

Question. 2.44: *Assume the same facts as Question 2.43. Also assume that the executor of Martin's estate wishes to avoid paying income taxes on the estate income tax return on the entire $14,200 that he must receive from Martin's IRA during 2008. The estate has additional income, all of which is tax exempt. What options are available to the executor of the estate of Martin in order to save income taxes?*

Answer: The professional advisor to Martin's estate should suggest to the executor that the estate of Martin select a fiscal year so that the entire $14,200 is not received in one tax year. The estate is subject to high federal income tax rates at relatively low levels of estate taxable income. It is important to minimize taxable income where possible since a significant portion of estate taxable income is subject to a 39.6% federal income tax rate. In addition, the estate may be subject to state income taxes as well. It is possible to have the $7,000 IRA distribution attributable to the calendar year 2007 received in one fiscal year of the estate and the $7,200 IRA distribution attributable to calendar year 2008 received in another fiscal year of the estate through proper planning.

In addition, distributions if timely made by Martin's executor to the beneficiaries of Martin's estate will shift the income tax burden from the estate to the beneficiaries of the estate. This should be done if the beneficiaries of the estate are in a lower income tax bracket than the estate. Generally, most beneficiaries are in a lower income tax bracket than the estate.

CHAPTER 3

Choosing Your Spouse as Your Designated Beneficiary

Tax planning and estate planning are crucial when you select a designated beneficiary. If your spouse is the designated beneficiary of a qualified plan, a 403(b) annuity contract, or an IRA, then both you and your spouse must become familiar with the special distribution rules discussed in this chapter.

The tax law favors spousal beneficiaries with tax-savings opportunities not available to other beneficiaries. For example, the restrictive life expectancy "MDIB" rules that apply to younger beneficiaries (see Chapter 4) do not apply to spousal beneficiaries. The life expectancy of a spousal beneficiary may be recalculated annually but not that of other beneficiaries. After the owner's death, a surviving spouse is the only beneficiary that may roll over the deceased's account to an IRA in the survivor's own name.

If you are married and do not plan to select your spouse as the designated beneficiary of your IRA or qualified plan death benefits, be aware that many qualified plans require that the surviving spouse receive all or at least a portion of the plan death benefits. However, a spouse may waive his or her rights to these plan death benefits. IRAs are not subject to spousal rights under the federal law. However, state law may grant the surviving spouse certain rights to IRA death benefits.

Your First Minimum Required Distribution:

The following questions and answers highlight the rules that apply when you name your spouse as your designated beneficiary and you must start to receive required minimum distributions at your required beginning date following the attainment of age $70^{1}/_{2}$.

Question 3.1: *Frank Wagner has an IRA at the ABC Bank. His 70th birthday is on March 15, 1998 and he attains age $70^{1}/_{2}$ on September 15, 1998. His wife, Cathy, the designated beneficiary of his IRA, is age 67 on November 15, 1998. When must Frank receive his first required minimum distribution from his IRA?*

Answer: The first year for which Frank must receive a minimum distribution, his "first distribution calendar year," is 1998, the calendar year in which he attains age $70^{1}/_{2}$. However, for the first distribution calendar year, the tax law allows extra time to take the minimum required distribution. Frank must receive his required minimum distribution for his first distribution calendar year 1998 by no later than April 1, 1999. Frank's required beginning date is April 1, 1999.

Question 3.2: *If Frank wants to base his minimum required distributions on his joint life expectancy with Cathy, what should he do?*

Answer: Frank must select Cathy as his designated beneficiary by his required beginning date of April 1, 1999, in order to base his required distributions on their joint life expectancy.

Question 3.3: *How is the joint life expectancy of Frank and Cathy determined?*

Answer: The joint life expectancy of Frank and Cathy is based upon their attained ages in the year that Frank reached age 70¹/₂. Frank attained age 70¹/₂ on September 15, 1998. Frank is age 70 and Cathy is age 67 in 1998. Under the IRS joint life expectancy Table II shown in the Appendix of this book, the joint life expectancy of a 70- and 67-year-old is 22 years.

Question 3.4: *Assume that Frank timely selected his wife, Cathy, as the designated beneficiary of his IRA. How much is Frank's required minimum distribution for his first distribution calendar year 1998?*

Answer: Frank must divide his and Cathy's joint life expectancy into his IRA account balance as of the end of the year prior to the first distribution calendar year. Since 1998 is the first distribution calendar year, the account balance as of December 31, 1997 must be used. Assume Frank's IRA account balance on December 31, 1997 is $100,000.

Frank's required minimum distribution for his first distribution calendar year 1998 is $4,545.45. This amount is determined as follows:

Frank's IRA account balance as of December 31, 1997	$100,000.00
Divided by the joint life expectancy of Frank and Cathy for the calendar year 1998	÷ 22 years
Required minimum distribution for the calendar year 1998	$4,545.45

For the year 1998, Frank must receive a minimum of $4545.45 to satisfy the IRS rules. He may of course withdraw more than that. Whatever he receives from the IRA will be taxable in the year of receipt.

Question 3.5: *May Frank receive his required minimum distribution for his first distribution calendar year 1998 in 1998?*

Answer: Yes. Frank may receive his required minimum distribution for his first distribution calendar year in 1998. He may receive it at any time during the period between January 1, 1998 and April 1, 1999. Frank's required beginning date is April 1, 1999.

Question 3.6: *Assume that Frank has other IRAs as well as a profit-sharing plan account under his employer's plan. The profit-sharing plan is on a calendar year basis. Does Frank have to receive a required minimum distribution from each of these arrangements by his required beginning date of April 1, 1999?*

Answer: Yes. Frank must receive required minimum distributions for the year 1998, his first distribution calendar year. For each of his IRAs, Frank must compute a required minimum distribution based upon the account balance of each IRA as of December 31, 1997, following the steps shown in Question 3.4. However, the required minimum distributions from all of the IRAs may be received from any one IRA, or any combination of IRAs, as Frank prefers. The plan administrator of Frank's profit-sharing plan will calculate a required minimum distribution, following the same steps, and make the distribution to Frank. However, see the answer to Question 2.3 for proposed legislation that would allow a delay if Frank is still working.

Term-Certain Method:

The following questions and answers explain how election of the term-certain method affects the calculation of required minimum distributions.

Question 3.7: *Assume that the IRA plan document permits Frank to elect the term-certain method of calculating his required minimum distributions for both he and his wife. What term-certain period is applicable to Frank if Cathy has been timely selected as his designated beneficiary?*

Answer: Frank may elect a term-certain period based upon his and Cathy's joint life expectancy as determined in the calendar year 1998.

Based upon an initial joint life expectancy of 22 years (see Question 3.3) in 1998, the term-certain period used to calculate the required distribution for each distribution calendar year will decrease by one each year—from 22 to 21 to 20 to 19 and so on.

The mechanics of electing the term-certain method were discussed in Questions 2.27 through 2.29, in Chapter 2. A joint term-certain election is permissible in most IRA plan documents.

Question 3.8: *Assume that Frank timely selected Cathy as his designated beneficiary and timely elected the term-certain method of calculating his required minimum distributions. Assume that Cathy dies in the calendar year 2005. The calendar year 2005 is Frank's eighth distribution calendar year. May Frank continue to use the balance of the initial term-certain period of 22 years in determining his required minimum distributions?*

Answer: Yes. If the IRA owner timely elects a term-certain method of calculating his required minimum distributions, that method will survive the death of the designated beneficiary. If Cathy dies during the term-certain period Frank can still continue to use the balance of the initial term-certain period. Thus, Frank will determine his required minimum distribution for his ninth distribution calendar year 2006 by dividing his IRA account balance as of December 31, 2005 by 14 years, the unused balance of the initial 22-year term-certain period. Frank can still continue to use the balance of the term-certain period for all later years as well. Upon his subsequent death his beneficiary can still continue to use the balance of the term-certain period. A partial listing of the term-certain period follows.

Term-Certain	Year	Period
First distribution calendar year	1998	22
Second distribution calendar year	1999	21
Third distribution calendar year	2000	20
Fourth distribution calendar year	2001	19
Fifth distribution calendar year	2002	18
Sixth distribution calendar year	2003	17
Seventh distribution calendar year	2004	16
Eighth distribution calendar year	2005	15
Ninth distribution calendar year	2006	14

Question 3.9: *Assume that Frank timely selected Cathy as his designated beneficiary and timely elected the term-certain method of calculating his required minimum distributions. Also assume that he did not specify the term-certain period in his election with the IRA institution. May Frank use the 22-year term-certain period?*

Answer: Yes. The IRS does not require that the term-certain period be spelled out. It is best to spell it out but it is not a legal requirement. The 22-year period based upon Frank and Cathy's joint life expectancy would be automatically available.

Question 3.10: *Assume that Frank timely selected Cathy as his designated beneficiary and timely elected the term-certain method of calculating his required minimum distributions. Also assume that Frank dies on August 1, 2003, having already received his required minimum distribution for the calendar year 2003. The calendar year 2003 is Frank's sixth distribution calendar year. Assume that Cathy survives Frank. May Cathy receive distributions from Frank's IRA for the balance remaining in the initial term-certain period, which is 16 years?*

Answer: Yes. Cathy may receive the balance in Frank's IRA over 16 years, the balance of the initial 22-year term-certain period.

Question 3.11: *Assume the same facts in Question 3.10, except that Cathy was advised shortly after Frank's death to create a spousal IRA rollover account. Should Cathy make the rollover?*

Answer: Yes. There is an advantage in making the spousal rollover. By rolling over the account to a new spousal IRA rollover account in her own name, Cathy can select her own designated beneficiary. This may allow Cathy to spread out distributions from the spousal IRA rollover account over a period that is longer than 16 years, the balance of Frank's initial term-certain period.

Question 3.12: *Does Cathy's age at the time of Frank's death bar her from creating a spousal IRA rollover account?*

Answer: No. According to the IRS, the fact that Cathy has passed her required beginning date does not prevent her from creating a spousal IRA rollover account.

Question 3.13: *Assume the same facts in Question 3.10 and that Cathy was advised shortly after Frank's death to create a spousal IRA rollover account. Cathy creates a spousal IRA rollover account on September 1, 2003. Cathy is age 72 on November 15, 2003. Cathy immediately selects her son, Thomas, as the designated beneficiary of her spousal IRA rollover. Thomas is age 40 on April 15, 2003. Must Cathy receive a required minimum distribution during the calendar year 2003 from this new spousal IRA rollover account that she created in the calendar year 2003?*

Answer: No. According to the IRS, if the IRA owner in the calendar year of death received his or her required minimum distribution, then the designated beneficiary need not receive a required minimum distribution in the same calendar year that the IRA owner died.

Question 3.14: *Assume that Frank timely selected Cathy as his designated beneficiary and timely elected the term-certain method of calculating his required minimum distributions. Also assume that Frank died on August 1, 2003 before he received his required minimum distribution of $10,000 for the calendar year 2003. Cathy would like to create a spousal IRA rollover in the calendar year 2003 of Frank's entire account balance of $110,000. May Cathy create a spousal IRA rollover of $110,000?*

Answer: No. The IRS does not permit Cathy to roll over a required minimum distribution. Cathy may create a spousal IRA rollover to the extent of $100,000 not $110,000. She must report the required minimum distribution of $10,000 as income in 2003. Cathy should not roll over Frank's IRA account into her own preexisting IRA account.

Question 3.15: *If, before his death in 2003, Frank receives his required minimum distribution for 2003, and Cathy creates a spousal IRA rollover account on September 1, 2003, when does Cathy have to commence her required minimum distributions from her spousal IRA rollover account?*

Answer: The IRS recognizes that Cathy has already attained her required beginning date as of the date of the creation of the spousal IRA rollover account. In that situation, according to the IRS she must commence her required minimum distributions from her spousal IRA rollover account in the calendar year following Frank's year of death. Since Frank died in the calendar year 2003, Cathy must commence her required minimum distributions from her spousal IRA rollover account during the calendar year 2004.

Question 3.16: *If Cathy creates a spousal IRA rollover account as discussed in Question 3.13, and names her son, Thomas, as beneficiary, how is Cathy's required minimum distribution from her spousal IRA rollover account for the calendar year 2004 determined?*

Answer: Cathy is age 73 in the calendar year 2004, and Thomas, the designated beneficiary of the spousal IRA rollover account, is age 41 in the calendar year 2004. Since Cathy has passed her required beginning date and has a non-spouse designated beneficiary who is more than 10 years younger than she is, then Cathy is subject to the special MDIB rules discussed in Chapter 4. Under the MDIB rules, Thomas' actual age may not be used during Cathy's lifetime to determine joint life expectancy. Instead, Thomas during Cathy's lifetime is considered to be 10 years younger than Cathy. As a result, Cathy must use ages 73 (her age in 2004) and 63 (Thomas' deemed age under MDIB rules) when looking up their joint life expectancy in the IRS tables. As shown in the table in the Appendix, the joint life expectancy for a 73-year-old and 63-year-old is 23.5 years. For the calendar year 2005, Cathy must use age 74 (her age in 2005 and 64—Thomas' deemed age under MDIB rule).

The IRS has a special table as shown in the Appendix that automatically calculates the joint life expectancy based upon a non-spouse designated beneficiary who is more than 10 years younger than the IRA owner. The table can be found in the Appendix to this book; it is from IRS Publication 590, Appendix E. It is called the Table for Determining Applicable Diviser for MDIB (Minimum Distribution Incidental Benefit).

The MDIB rule is not applicable in calendar years after Cathy's subsequent death. The age of Thomas is taken into account in calendar years after Cathy's death. This is explained in Chapter 4.

The special MDIB rule is not considered to be a recalculation method or a term-certain method. It is considered to be a special computation.

Question 3.17: *How much is Cathy's required minimum distribution from the spousal IRA rollover account for the calendar year 2004?*

Answer: Assuming that the value of the spousal IRA rollover account balance at the end of 2003 is $105,000, Cathy's required minimum distribution for the calendar year 2004 year would be $4,468.09. This amount is determined as follows:

Cathy's spousal IRA rollover account balance as of December 31, 2003	$ 105,000
Divided by the applicable divisor for the calendar year 2004	÷ 23.5 years
Required minimum distribution for the calendar year 2004	$ 4,468.09

Question 3.18: *Based upon the fact that at the time of Frank's death he has passed his required beginning date and Cathy has passed her required beginning date, when should Cathy select the designated beneficiary of her spousal IRA rollover account?*

Answer: Based upon the fact that Frank died after his required beginning date, Cathy should select the designated beneficiary of her spousal IRA rollover account as soon as possible in order to reduce her required minimum distributions and provide for an extended payout for her designated beneficiary.

According to the IRS, since Frank died after his required beginning date Cathy must select the designated beneficiary of her spousal IRA rollover account prior to December 31, 2004. This is prior to the last day of 2004, the year in which she must commence her required minimum distributions from her spousal IRA rollover account. If Frank had died prior to his required beginning date, then Cathy could create the spousal IRA rollover account by the later of December 31 of the calendar year following Frank's death or December 31 of the calendar year in which Frank would have attained $70^1/_2$ had he lived.

This is a crucial issue because if Cathy should die before she consummates the spousal IRA rollover account and if the recalculation method is applicable, then under the recalculation method Frank's entire IRA account balance must be paid to Cathy's estate by December 30 of the calendar year following the year of her death. However, if Cathy immediately creates a spousal IRA rollover account and selects her son, Thomas, as the designated beneficiary of the spousal IRA rollover account, she could compute her required minimum distribution using the MDIB rules discussed in Question 3.16 and Chapter 4. If the term-certain method is applicable and Cathy dies before creating the spousal IRA rollover, then her estate may receive the required minimum distributions for the balance of the term-certain period. The recalculation method is discussed in Questions 3.25 through 3.34.

Question 3.19: *Is there any other reason that Cathy should select a designated beneficiary of her spousal IRA rollover account as soon as possible?*

Answer: Yes. Upon Cathy's subsequent death, her designated beneficiary, Thomas, for example, may take advantage of the extended payout rules discussed in Chapter 4 that are available to a nonspouse designated beneficiary who is more than 10 years younger than the IRA owner. If Cathy should die or become incompetent before she selects the designated beneficiary of her spousal IRA rollover account, then her estate becomes the beneficiary of her spousal IRA rollover account and the entire IRA account balance would have to be paid to her estate by December 30 of the calendar year following the year of Cathy's death under the recalculation method, unless the term-certain method was applicable.

Question 3.20: *May Cathy establish more than one spousal IRA rollover account?*

Answer: Yes. Upon Frank's death, Cathy may establish more than one spousal IRA rollover account and select a different designated beneficiary for each spousal IRA rollover account.

Question 3.21: *If Cathy creates more than one spousal IRA rollover account, must she receive her required minimum distributions from each IRA?*

Answer: No. The IRS permits Cathy to receive her total required minimum distribution from her IRAs for a particular calendar year from any IRA or combination of IRAs that she wishes.

Question 3.22: *Assume that Cathy has one regular IRA and one spousal IRA rollover account. Assume that during a given calendar year she must receive $2,500 as a required minimum distribution from the regular IRA and $5,000 as a required minimum distribution from her spousal IRA rollover account. May she receive the entire $7,500 from either IRA?*

Answer: Yes. The IRS permits Cathy to receive the $7,500 required minimum distribution for the given calendar year from any IRA she wishes. She may allocate the distribution entirely to one IRA or partially to one IRA and partially to the other IRA. These IRA distributions need not be allocated in any specific manner.

Question 3.23: *If under the facts of Question 3.11, Frank dies and Cathy decides to create a spousal IRA rollover account, but Cathy dies before she can establish the account, would the executor of her estate be able to set up the spousal IRA rollover account?*

Answer: No. Only a surviving spouse can create a spousal IRA rollover. An executor has no authority under the tax law to do so.

Question 3.24: *Based upon the facts in Question 3.23 may Cathy's estate receive the balance in Frank's IRA over the remaining term-certain period of 16 years that is left in the initial 22-year term-certain period?*

Answer: Yes. Since the spousal IRA rollover was never made, Cathy's estate may continue to use the remaining 16-year period in determining its required minimum distributions from Frank's IRA.

Recalculation Method:

The following questions and answers explain how required minimum distributions are calculated under the recalculation method of determining life expectancy.

Question 3.25: *What is the recalculation method?*

Answer: The recalculation method allows the IRA owner who has timely selected a spousal designated beneficiary, to use their attained age as of their birthday in each year when looking up their joint life expectancy in the IRS tables. The effect of this "recalculation" is that joint life expectancy decreases by less than one in each succeeding year.

Question 3.26: *Assume that an IRA owner selects his or her spouse as the designated beneficiary by no later than the required beginning date. Also assume that under the IRA plan document, the recalculation method of determining life expectancy is the default option if another method is not elected. Would this default option apply to both the IRA owner and his or her spouse as the designated beneficiary?*

Answer: Yes. If the IRA owner timely selected his or her spouse as the designated beneficiary and fails to elect out of the recalculation method by the required beginning date, then the recalculation method is applicable to both the IRA owner and the designated spousal beneficiary under the default option.

Question 3.27: *How does IRA owner determine whether or not the default option into the recalculation method is applicable?*

Answer: The majority of IRA plan documents state that unless the IRA owner elects out of the recalculation method by his or her required beginning date, the recalculation method applies as the default option.

Question 3.28: *Does the recalculation method apply to a non-spouse who is selected as the designated beneficiary?*

Answer: No. A nonspouse designated beneficiary is not allowed to recalculate life expectancy. This is true even if the owner does recalculate. Where the owner does recalculate, a special method must be used to calculate joint life expectancy, as shown in Chapter 4.

Question 3.29: *Assume that Frank Wagner, an IRA owner, is age 70 on March 15, 1998 and age 70½ on September 15, 1998. Frank's required beginning date is April 1, 1999. His wife,*

Cathy, the designated beneficiary of his IRA, is age 67 on November 15, 1998. Frank elects to recalculate his and Cathy's life expectancy. Assume that Frank and Cathy are alive during the calendar years 1998 through 2008. Would you please show what life expectancy Frank would use for the calendar years 1998 through 2008 under the recalculation method in determining his required minimum distributions from his IRA?

Answer: The following schedule shows the life expectancy that Frank would use under the recalculation method through 2008, when he would be age 80.

Recalculation of Life Expectancy

Frank's Age	Cathy's Age	Calendar Year	Distribution Year	Joint Life Expectancy Recalculation Method
70	67	1998	1	22.0
71	68	1999	2	21.2
72	69	2000	3	20.3
73	70	2001	4	19.4
74	71	2002	5	18.6
75	72	2003	6	17.8
76	73	2004	7	17.0
77	74	2005	8	16.2
78	75	2006	9	15.4
79	76	2007	10	14.7
80	77	2008	11	14.0

Question 3.30: *Assume that Frank timely selected Cathy as the designated beneficiary of his IRA. Would you compare the life expectancy period that Frank may use under the recalculation method with the life expectancy that may be used under the term-certain method during the calendar years 1998 through 2008?*

Answer: The following schedule indicates the difference between the life expectancy that Frank would use during the calendar year 1998 through 2008 under each method.

As the schedule indicates life expectancy is reduced more slowly under the recalculation method. As a result, slightly smaller annual distributions are required under the recalculation method than under the term-certain method.

Recalculation Method vs. Term-Certain Method

Frank's Age	Cathy's Age	Calendar Year	Distribution Year	Joint Life Expectancy Term-Certain Method	Joint Life Expectancy Recalculation Method
70	67	1998	1	22	22.0
71	68	1999	2	21	21.2
72	69	2000	3	20	20.3
73	70	2001	4	19	19.4
74	71	2002	5	18	18.6
75	72	2003	6	17	17.8
76	73	2004	7	16	17.0
77	74	2005	8	15	16.2
78	75	2006	9	14	15.4
79	76	2007	10	13	14.7
80	77	2008	11	12	14.0

Question 3.31: *Assume the facts in Question 3.29 except that Cathy dies in 2003. How does her death affect the life expectancy Frank must use under the recalculation method in figuring his subsequent required minimum distributions for the calendar years 2004 through 2008?*

Answer: Since Cathy died in the calendar year 2003, her life expectancy under the recalculation method becomes zero in the calendar year after her death. For 2003, the year of her death, Frank figures his required minimum distribution using a joint life expectancy of 17.8 years, the same as if Cathy were alive. In the year 2004, Frank must use only his own single life expectancy of 11.9 years. IRS Table I in the Appendix shows 11.9 years as the single life expectancy for an individual age 76.

For later years, here is the single life expectancy Frank would use:

Single

Frank's Age	Calendar Year	Distribution Year	Life Expectancy
77	2005	8	11.2
78	2006	9	10.6
79	2007	10	10.0
80	2008	11	9.5

Question 3.32: *Assume the facts in Question 3.31 except that Frank after Cathy's death names his son, Thomas, as the new designated beneficiary of his IRA. Does this change the answer to Question 3.31?*

Answer: No. The recalculation method cannot be changed after the required beginning date. The substitution of a new designated beneficiary after the death of Cathy will not permit Frank to avoid the recalculation method.

Frank must continue to use his single life expectancy each year when figuring his required minimum distributions, regardless of who he may name as the replacement beneficiary of his IRA.

Question 3.33: *Assume the facts in Question 3.29 except that Frank a few days before Cathy's death changes the designated beneficiary of his IRA from Cathy to his son, Thomas. Will your answers to Questions 3.31 and 3.32 change?*

Answer: No. The IRS position is that if you change your designated beneficiary after your required beginning date from an older to a younger designated beneficiary, you must continue to use the life expectancy of the original, older designated beneficiary. If Frank replaced Cathy with Thomas as his designated beneficiary, he would still have to treat Cathy as the designated beneficiary for purposes of calculating his required minimum distributions. After Cathy dies, her life expectancy is reduced to zero in the calendar year following the year of her death, as explained in Question 3.31. The fact that Thomas was the designated beneficiary when Cathy dies does not change this result.

Question 3.34: *Assume the facts in Question 3.31 except that Frank names his estate as the beneficiary of his IRA after Cathy's death in 2003. Frank dies in 2006 after receiving his required minimum distribution for 2006. When must Frank's estate receive Frank's IRA account balance?*

Answer: Frank's estate must receive Frank's entire IRA account balance by no later than December 30, 2007. Under the recalculation method Frank's life expectancy is reduced to zero in 2007, the calendar year following the year of his death. Cathy's life expectancy has already been reduced to zero in the calendar year 2004. According to the IRS, for any calendar year in which the last applicable life expectancy is reduced to zero, the entire IRA account balance (including earnings or decreased by losses) must be distributed prior to the last day of such calendar year. Therefore, Frank's estate must receive the entire account balance between the period January 1, 2007 and December 30, 2007.

Question 3.35: *Assume the facts in Question 3.34 except that Frank had timely selected the term-certain method of receiving his required minimum distributions from his IRA instead of the recalculation method. Also assume that Frank's IRA balance as of December 31, 2006 is $300,000. Must Frank's estate receive his entire IRA account balance during the period January 1, 2007 through December 30, 2007?*

Answer: No. Since Frank timely elected the term-certain method of receiving his required minimum distributions from his IRA, then his estate may succeed to the remaining period that is left in the initial term-certain period of 22 years. During the calendar year 2007 the required minimum distribution that Frank's estate must receive is $23,076.92. This is determined as follows:

Frank's IRA account balance as of December 31, 2006	$ 300,000.00
Divided by the remaining period left in the term-certain period as of the calendar year 2007	÷ 13 years
Required minimum distribution for the calendar year 2007	$23,076.92

Under the term-certain method the required minimum distribution must be received by Frank's estate during the period January 1, 2007 through December 31, 2007.

Lump-Sum Death Benefits Paid by an Employer Plan to Surviving Spouse:

The following questions and answers discuss the tax planning options of a surviving spouse who is entitled to receive a lump-sum payment from a qualified employer retirement plan following the death of his or her spouse.

Question 3.36: *Ronald Kane is a participant in a qualified profit-sharing plan. His wife, Linda, is his designated beneficiary. The plan provides that a lump-sum distribution of his death benefits in the plan be paid to her within one year after his death. Ronald dies in 1998 at the age of 64. The lump sum is approximately $100,000. Linda is age 62 in 1998. What options are available to Linda?*

Answer: Linda may receive a lump-sum distribution from the qualified plan and elect special averaging treatment or she may arrange for the plan death benefits to be transferred directly to a brand new IRA that she establishes in her own name.

Question 3.37: *Why should Linda consider using special averaging treatment?*

Answer: If Linda has substantial taxable income and is in a high tax bracket, special averaging can greatly reduce the tax liability on the lump-sum distribution. For example, if Linda is in the 31% tax bracket, the use of special averaging treatment will cut the income tax liability down to approximately 15%.

Question 3.38: *What type of special averaging treatment are we talking about?*

Answer: There are two methods of calculating the income tax liability on a lump-sum distribution from a qualified plan. These methods are five-year special averaging treatment and 10-year special averaging treatment. Since Ronald Kane, the plan participant, was born before 1936, then Linda as his beneficiary may elect special 10-year averaging treatment using the 1986 federal tax rates, or, if more advantageous, five-year averaging using the federal income tax rates for single persons in the year the distribution is received.

If Ronald had not been born before 1936, but had died on or after age $59^1/_2$, then his beneficiary could use five-year averaging, but not 10-year averaging, to compute the tax on the lump-sum distribution.

It is possible that Congress may eliminate the option of claiming special averaging for individuals not born before 1936. In fact, such legislation was being considered by Congress when this book went to press.

Question 3.39: *If Linda has the option to use either five-year special averaging treatment or 10-year special averaging treatment, which method should she use?*

Answer: Since Ronald Kane was born before 1936, Linda may use 10-year averaging treatment or she may use five-year averaging. The tax liability is practically the same at the $100,000 level. The income tax on $100,000 under 10-year averaging is $14,471 and at five-year averaging is $15,000. The averaging computation is made on IRS Form 4972. These amounts do not consider the $5,000 death benefit exclusion that may be available as an offset against the $100,000 lump-sum distribution.

Question 3.40: *What is the death benefit exclusion all about?*

Answer: At the time this book went to press, The Internal Revenue Code permitted up to $5,000 of death benefits to be excluded from taxable income. However, the same proposed legislation mentioned in the answer to Question 3.38 that would repeal five-year averaging would also repeal the $5,000 death benefit exclusion.

Question 3.41: *Assume that Ronald Kane was born on June 1, 1937 and died on May 10, 1996 at age 58. May Linda Kane use special averaging treatment?*

Answer: No. Since Ronald Kane was not born before 1936, Linda Kane may not use special 10-year averaging treatment as his beneficiary. Congress may repeal five-year averaging for those born after 1935, but even if it does not do so, Linda could not use five-year averaging since Ronald died prior to age $59^1/_2$.

Question 3.42: *If Linda may not claim special averaging based upon the facts in Question 3.41, what should she do?*

Answer: Linda should consider transferring the death benefits directly to a brand new IRA. She would do this by instructing the plan administrator of Ronald's account to transfer the account directly to an IRA that she has selected.

If, however, the $5,000 death benefit exclusion is still available under the law, then only $95,000 should be transferred directly to a brand new IRA. The $5,000 death benefit exclusion should be received directly by her since that amount is tax free. If the law is changed and the $5,000 death benefit exclusion is eliminated, then $100,000 should be transferred directly to a brand new IRA.

Question 3.43: *In your answer to Question 3.42, you suggest transferring the $95,000 directly to a brand new IRA. Why should the $95,000 be transferred directly to a new IRA?*

Answer: A direct transfer avoids the mandatory 20% withholding requirement. When a distribution is made from a qualified employer retirement plan to the plan participant or to his or her spousal beneficiary, 20% must be withheld.

If the plan administrator is instructed to make a direct transfer to an IRA or another qualified plan, there is no tax on the transfer and no withholding.

It is best that the transfer be made to a brand new IRA instead of a pre-existing IRA for several technical reasons. For example, state law may provide that IRAs created as a result of the receipt of monies from a qualified plan are protected against creditors. There are several other reasons for the creation of a new IRA that are discussed in this book.

Question 3.44: *Assume that Ronald's employer awards Linda an additional corporate death benefit (not life insurance) of $5,000 as a widow's death benefit. May Linda exclude $10,000 as a death benefit?*

Answer: No. The law only permits an aggregate death benefit amount of $5,000 to be excluded with respect to the decedent. The IRS requires that the death benefit exclusion of $5,000 be allocated between the $100,000 plan death benefit and the $5,000 widow's death benefit.

Thus, $4,761.90 of the death benefit exclusion is allocated to the plan death benefit, and $238.10 is allocated to the widow's death benefit received from the employer.

Surviving Spouse's Rollover of IRA:

If an IRA owner dies before the required beginning date, and his or her spouse is the designated beneficiary, then the surviving spouse has the option of rolling over the funds to one or more new IRAs in his or her name, as discussed in the following questions and answers.

Question 3.45: *Roger Smith is age 62 in 1998. He has an IRA account with the XYZ bank that contains approximately $75,000. Jane Smith, his wife, is the designated beneficiary of Roger's IRA account. Jane is age 60 in 1998. Assume that Roger dies in 1999. Jane does not need the income and would like to defer paying taxes on these funds at the present time. What options are available to Jane?*

Answer: Jane may treat Roger's IRA account as her own or she can be taxed under the designated beneficiary rules that are applicable to a surviving spouse.

Question 3.46: *Which approach is best for Jane?*

Answer: As Jane does not have a current need for the funds, she should definitely treat the IRA account as her own for estate and tax planning reasons.

Question 3.47: *How does Jane make the IRA account her own?*

Answer: Jane may merely change the title of the IRA account to her own name or request a distribution from the IRA institution and roll it over into a brand new spousal IRA rollover account in her name. A roll over to a new spousal IRA rollover must be completed within 60 days of the date that Jane receives the distribution from Roger's IRA.

Question 3.48: *Must Jane create only one spousal IRA rollover account?*

Answer: No. Jane may roll over the IRA distribution from Roger's IRA into as many spousal IRA rollover accounts as she wishes.

Question 3.49: *How does Jane create multiple spousal IRA rollover accounts?*

Answer: Jane must complete the spousal rollover within 60 days from the date that she receives the initial distribution from her deceased spouse's IRA account. Jane can deposit the funds that she receives from Roger's IRA into her own money market account. She can then within the 60-day period from the date that she receives the initial distribution from Roger's IRA transfer the initial distribution amount into multiple spousal IRA rollover accounts.

Question 3.50: *Assume Jane receives the IRA death benefits from Roger's IRA and temporarily transfers these funds into her money market account. Assume she earns $500 on these funds while they are in the money market account. May she transfer these earnings into a spousal IRA rollover account?*

Answer: No. Only the initial amount she receives may be timely transferred into a spousal IRA rollover account. She may, of course, timely transfer the initial amount into more than one spousal IRA rollover account.

Question 3.51: *Are distributions from IRAs subject to the 20% federal withholding tax requirement?*

Answer: No. Distributions from IRAs are not subject to the mandatory 20% withholding requirement that applies to distributions from a qualified employer plan (Question 3.43).

IRA distributions are subject to withholding, generally at a 10% rate, but an election to avoid this withholding can be filed with the IRA trustee.

Question 3.52: *When should Jane consummate the spousal IRA rollover?*

Answer: Jane should act promptly after Roger's death and create the spousal IRA rollover account(s). The reason that this prompt action is necessary is because only a surviving spouse can create a spousal IRA rollover account. If Jane should die before she creates the spousal IRA rollover, then her executor may not create the spousal IRA rollover account.

Question 3.53: *Why is it important that the surviving spouse act quickly in establishing the spousal IRA rollover?*

Answer: Jane can use a spousal IRA rollover as a tool in her retirement distribution planning. Jane may create multiple spousal IRA rollovers and select a different member of the family as the designated beneficiary of each spousal IRA rollover account. The life expectancy of the designated beneficiary as well as the income tax bracket of the designated beneficiary should be considered in order to maximize the tax benefits of the spousal IRA rollover accounts.

Surviving Spouse Option to Receive IRA Distributions as Beneficiary:

If an IRA owner dies before his required beginning date and the surviving spouse elects not to treat the deceased spouse's IRA as his or her own, then special rules for electing the life expectancy rule and commencing distributions may be available, as discussed in the following questions and answers.

Question 3.54: *Sheldon Madison was born on June 15, 1937. He dies on August 10, 1998 at age 61. His wife, Darlene Madison, is age 48 on January 20, 1998. Darlene is the designated beneficiary of Sheldon's IRA. What options are available to Darlene?*

Answer: Darlene has several options. She may treat Sheldon's IRA as her own or she can be taxed under the designated beneficiary rules that are applicable to a surviving spouse.

Question 3.55: *Darlene wants as much flexibility as possible in being able to withdraw funds from Sheldon's IRA. Her primary interest is in avoiding exposure to the 10% early distribution penalty. Should she consider receiving distributions under the designated beneficiary rules instead of creating a spousal IRA rollover account?*

Answer: Yes, unless she qualifies for an exception that was previously discussed in Chapter 1. Since Darlene is age 48 when Sheldon dies, she would be subject to the 10% early distribution penalty if she created a spousal IRA rollover account and took withdrawals from the IRA before reaching age $59^{1}/_{2}$. However, if she withdraws funds from Sheldon's IRA under the designated beneficiary rules, the 10% penalty does not apply.

Question 3.56: *Assume that Darlene's date of birth is January 20, 1950. She will attain age $59^{1}/_{2}$ on July 20, 2009. May Darlene receive distributions from Sheldon's IRA as a designated beneficiary from time to time during the period between Sheldon's date of death of August 10, 1998 and July 20, 2009 without worrying about the 10% early distribution penalty?*

Answer: Yes. Since Darlene is receiving distributions from Sheldon's IRA in her capacity as a designated beneficiary, then she is not subject to the 10% early distribution penalty if she receives IRA death benefits. It does not matter whether or not Darlene is under age $59^{1}/_{2}$ at the time she receives distributions from Sheldon's IRA in her capacity as a designated beneficiary.

Question 3.57: *Could Darlene elect to receive distributions from Sheldon's IRA for a number of years under the designated beneficiary rules, in order to avoid the 10% early distribution penalty, and later rollover the account to an IRA in her own name?*

Answer: Yes, Darlene may receive distributions before she attains age $59^{1}/_{2}$ from Sheldon's IRA as a designated beneficiary and avoid the 10% early distribution penalty. She can at a later date create a spousal IRA rollover and treat the IRA account as her own. This should be done prior to the time that the designated beneficiary distribution rules are triggered.

Alternatively, Darlene may decide to immediately use a split approach. For example, if Sheldon's IRA account balance at the date of his death was $150,000, and Darlene wanted to withdraw $100,000 prior to the time she attained age 59^1/$_2$, Darlene could create a spousal IRA rollover for approximately $50,000 within a few months after Sheldon's death. This spousal IRA rollover account would not be subject to the designated beneficiary distribution rules that are applicable to a surviving spouse. The remaining $100,000 in Sheldon's IRA account plus the earnings thereon would be subject to the designated beneficiary rules that are applicable to a surviving spouse. Darlene would therefore avoid the 10% early distribution penalty on the distributions she receives prior to age 59^1/$_2$ under the designated beneficiary rules on the amount that she does not roll over.

Question 3.58: *Under the distribution rules for designated beneficiaries, what method would Darlene use to withdraw funds from Sheldon's IRA?*

Answer: It depends on whether the IRA plan document requires use of the so-called five-year rule. Under the five-year rule, the entire balance of a deceased IRA owner's account balance must be paid to the designated beneficiary by no later than December 31 of the fifth year following the year of the IRA owner's death.

However, under an exception to the five-year rule, the IRA plan document may allow the designated beneficiary to elect to receive required minimum distributions over his or her life expectancy. The following questions and answers illustrate how the life expectancy method rules apply to a surviving spouse.

Question 3.59: *If an IRA owner dies before the required beginning date, and his or her surviving spouse is the designated beneficiary of the IRA, may the IRA plan document provide that the life expectancy exception to the five-year rule is automatic?*

Answer: Yes. The IRA plan document may provide that the exception to the five-year rule is automatic if the IRA owner dies before the required beginning date, leaving a surviving spouse as his or her designated beneficiary.

Question 3.60: *If the IRA plan document is silent on whether or not the five-year rule is applicable to a surviving spouse who is the designated beneficiary, does the five-year rule apply?*

Answer: No. According to the IRS, if the IRA plan document is silent, the life expectancy exception to the five-year rule is automatic where the designated beneficiary is the surviving spouse.

Question 3.61: *Assume that Darlene does not intend to treat Sheldon's IRA as her own. Darlene would like to use the designated beneficiary rules that are applicable to a surviving* *spouse. If the life expectancy exception to the five-year rule applies automatically to a surviving spouse under the IRA plan document, when must Darlene commence distributions from Sheldon's IRA under the designated beneficiary rules?*

Answer: When an IRA owner dies before the required beginning date, a special distribution commencement date applies to a surviving spouse. Distributions to Darlene must commence on or before the later of (1) December 31 of the year Sheldon would have reached age 70^1/$_2$ or (2) December 31 of the year following the year of Sheldon's death.

Sheldon died in 1998. If Sheldon had lived he would have attained age 70^1/$_2$ on December 15, 2007. Darlene must therefore commence distributions from Sheldon's IRA as a designated beneficiary by no later than December 31, 2007, as this date is later than December 31, 1999 (December 31 of the year after 1998, the year of death).

Question 3.62: *Assume that Sheldon's IRA plan document permits Darlene to elect whether the five-year rule or the life expectancy exception to the five-year rule is applicable. Assume that Darlene does not want to use the five-year rule. When must Darlene make the election out of the five-year rule?*

Answer: Special election rules apply to the surviving spouse. These rules are tied to the date of death of the IRA owner. Since Sheldon died on August 10, 1998 at age 61, then distributions to Darlene must commence by December 31, 2007; see the answer to Question 3.61. Darlene must elect out of the five-year rule by no later than the earlier of the December 31, 2007 commencement deadline, or December 31, 2003, the calendar year containing the fifth anniversary of Sheldon's death. The IRS allows Darlene to make the election out of the five-year rule by no later than the earlier date, which is December 31, 2003.

Therefore, in this case, Darlene's deadlines for electing the life expectancy rule, and for actually commencing distributions under that rule, are not the same. The election must be made by December 31, 2003, but distributions do not have to start until December 31, 2007.

Had Darlene been a nonspouse designated beneficiary, the election out of the five-year rule would have to be made no later than December 31st of the calendar year following the year of the IRA owner's death. By that same December 31st date, a nonspouse designated beneficiary must receive the first required minimum distribution under the life expectancy exception. See Chapter 8.

Question 3.63: *Assume that the terms of Sheldon's IRA plan document require Darlene to make an election out of the five-year rule in order to apply the life expectancy exception. How does Darlene make the election out of the five-year rule?*

Answer: Darlene should file a written election with the IRA institution that in essence states that she wishes to elect out of the five-year rule. The written election should be sent by certified mail, return receipt requested to the IRA institution. The written election should be made promptly after Sheldon's death on August 10, 1998. Darlene should not rely upon the extended dates for electing out of the five-year method as described in Question 3.62, since Darlene may forget to do it or be unable to make the election because of a physical or mental disability.

Question 3.64: *Assume that Darlene receives distributions from Sheldon's IRA in her capacity as a designated beneficiary and that the life expectancy exception to the five-year rule applies. What life expectancy table must Darlene use in determining her required minimum distributions from Sheldon's IRA.*

Answer: Darlene must use the IRS single life expectancy table under Table V of 1.72-9 of the Income Tax Regulations. This table, called Table I in IRS Publication 590, is shown in the Appendix of this book.

Question 3.65: *For purposes of figuring her first required minimum distribution from Sheldon's IRA, what is Darlene's life expectancy under the IRS single life expectancy table?*

Answer: Darlene must receive her first required minimum distribution from Sheldon's IRA by the end of 2007 (Question 3.61). If Darlene waits until 2007 to receive her first required minimum distribution, her age for purposes of determining her life expectancy is 57, her age on her birthday in 2007. As shown in the Appendix, Darlene has a single life expectancy at age 57 of 26.8 years. Darlene may use a single life expectancy of 26.8 years in calculating her required minimum distributions from Sheldon's IRA. Darlene must receive the first required minimum distribution from Sheldon's IRA in the calendar year 2007; see Question 3.61. She can, of course, receive distributions prior to the year 2007.

Question 3.66: *Assume that Sheldon's IRA account balance as of December 31, 2006 is $200,000. What is the amount of Darlene's required minimum distribution in her capacity as a designated beneficiary for the calendar year 2007?*

Answer: The amount of Darlene's required minimum distribution in her capacity as a designated beneficiary for the calendar year 2007 is $7,462.69. This is determined as follows:

Sheldon's IRA account balance as of December 31, 2006	$ 200,000.00
Divided by the single life expectancy of Darlene for the calendar year 2007 which is 26.8 (Question 3.65)	÷ 26.8
Required minimum distribution for the calendar year 2007	$7,462.69

Question 3.67: *Assume that Darlene withdrew $3,462.69 from Sheldon's IRA during the calendar year 2007 instead of $7,462.69. Can the IRS impose a penalty against Darlene for receiving less than the required amount?*

Answer: Yes. Darlene's required minimum distribution for the calendar year 2007 is $7,462.69. Since she only received $3,462.69, she is subject to a 50% penalty on the shortfall of $4,000. The penalty for the failure to receive a required minimum distribution is 50% of the shortfall or $2,000 in Darlene's case.

Question 3.68: *May the IRS waive the $2,000 penalty discussed in Question 3.67?*

Answer: Yes. The IRS may waive the 50% penalty if Darlene can prove to the IRS that she acted in a reasonable manner. In addition, as soon as she discovers the shortfall she must remedy the situation. If Darlene discovers the error in the calendar year 2008, she must immediately take an additional $4,000 distribution in the calendar year 2008 in addition to her required minimum distribution for the calendar year 2008.

Question 3.69: *Assume that Darlene withdraws $27,462.69 from Sheldon's IRA during the calendar year 2007 instead of the required minimum distribution of $7,462.69. Will Darlene receive a credit for the additional $20,000 distribution that she received in the calendar year 2007 against her required minimum distribution for the calendar year 2008?*

Answer: No. Darlene will not receive a credit of $20,000 against her required minimum distribution for the calendar year 2008. Although Darlene received substantially more than required in 2007, she must figure her required minimum distribution for 2008 under the regular rules, following the steps in Question 3.66, but using the account balance at the end of 2007 and a revised life expectancy. The revised life expectancy depends on whether the term-certain election is made or whether the recalculation method is applicable.

Question 3.70: *As you may recall, Sheldon died before his required beginning date. May Darlene use the recalculation method of determining life expectancy when figuring her minimum required distributions for the calendar year 2008 and subsequent years?*

Answer: Yes. The recalculation method may be used by a surviving spouse who is receiving distributions under the designated beneficiary rules.

Question 3.71: *Sheldon died before his required beginning date. May Darlene elect the term-certain method instead of the recalculation method?*

Answer: Perhaps. Most IRA plan documents permit the spouse to elect the term-certain method.

Question 3.72: *Assume that the IRA plan document permits Darlene to elect the term-certain method. When must Darlene elect the term-certain method?*

Answer: Darlene must elect the term-certain method by no later than the time of her first required minimum distribution. Since Darlene must receive her first required minimum distribution by the end of 2007, she must also elect the term-certain method with the IRA institution by no later than December 31, 2007.

Question 3.73: *How does Darlene elect the term-certain option?*

Answer: Darlene should send the IRA institution a written term-certain election. The written election should be sent to the IRA institution by registered mail, return receipt requested. The mechanics of making the election were previously discussed in Chapter 2.

Question 3.74: *Assume that Darlene dies in the calendar year 2015. Would you please compare the life expectancy period that Darlene would use under the term-certain method with the life expectancy that would be used if she recalculated life expectancy for the calendar years 2007 through 2015?*

Answer: The following schedule compares the two life expectancy methods for the calendar years 2007 through 2015.

Darlene's Age	Calendar Year	Term-certain Life Expectancy	Recalculation Method Life Expectancy
57	2007	26.8	26.8
58	2008	25.8	25.9
59	2009	24.8	25.0
60	2010	23.8	24.2
61	2011	22.8	23.3
62	2012	21.8	22.5
63	2013	20.8	21.6
64	2014	19.8	20.8
65	2015	18.8	20.0

As you can see, life expectancy is reduced more slowly under the recalculation method. As a result, slightly smaller required minimum distributions are required using the recalculation method.

Question 3.75: *If Darlene uses the recalculation method and she dies in the year 2015 after receiving her required minimum distribution for that year, over what period of time may Darlene's estate receive the balance in Sheldon's IRA?*

Answer: If the recalculation method is applicable, then Darlene's life expectancy is reduced to zero as of the calendar year 2016, the year following the year of her death. Darlene's estate must receive Sheldon's entire IRA account balance during the period January 1, 2016 and December 30, 2016.

Question 3.76: *Assume that the term-certain method is applicable and Darlene dies in the year 2015. Over what period may Darlene's estate receive the balance of Sheldon's IRA?*

Answer: If the term-certain method is applicable, then Darlene's estate may take advantage of the remaining period that is left in the initial 26.8-year term-certain period. As of the calendar year 2016 there are 17.8 years left in the initial term-certain period of 26.8 years. Darlene's estate or the beneficiaries of her estate may take advantage of the 17.8-year remaining term-certain period.

Question 3.77: *Assume that Sheldon had been born on June 15, 1931, instead of June 15, 1937 (Question 3.54), so that at his death on August 10, 1998, he is age 67. Based on these facts, when must Darlene make the election out of the five-year rule in order to receive distributions under the life expectancy exception?*

Answer: Sheldon would have attained age $70^1/_2$ on December 15, 2001 had he lived. Darlene must commence required minimum distributions under the exception to the five-year rule by no later than December 31, 2001. This is because December 31, 2001, the end of the year in which Sheldon would have reached age $70^1/_2$ had he lived, is later than December 31, 1999, the end of the year following 1998, Sheldon's year of death.

Darlene must elect out of the five-year rule by the earlier of the commencement date, December 31, 2001, or December 31, 2003, the end of the calendar year that contains the fifth anniversary of Sheldon's death. Since December 31, 2001 is the earlier date, that is the deadline for Darlene's election out of the five-year method. In addition, the term-certain election must be made by the commencement date, December 31, 2001.

Therefore, in this case, Darlene's deadlines for electing the life expectancy rule, and for actually commencing distributions are the same, December 31, 2001. Contrast this with the answer to Question 3.62, in which Darlene's deadline for electing out of the five-year rule is December 31, 2003, but the deadline for commencing her required distributions is December 31, 2007.

CHAPTER 4

Selecting a Child, Grandchild, or Other Young Person as Your Designated Beneficiary

As discussed in previous chapters, the timely selection of a designated beneficiary reduces the minimum annual distributions you are required to receive from your IRA, or from your employer's qualified plan, after you have reached your required beginning date. By taking into account the beneficiary's life expectancy as well as your own, you are able to "spread out" the distribution period over a longer period. For a person to be treated as your designated beneficiary, that person must be selected by no later than your required beginning date, which is April 1 of the year following the year in which you reach age 70^1/$_2$. However, certain exceptions and other rules may apply in certain situations. See Questions 2.3 and 3.18.

The tax law imposes a substantial limitation on your ability to extend the payment period by naming a younger beneficiary. If you name your child or grandchild as your designated beneficiary, you cannot use their actual age in determining your joint life expectancy. You must treat the beneficiary as being 10 years younger than you are, even if he or she is in fact much younger. This rule does not apply to a spouse.

The same rule also applies to any other designated beneficiary other than a spouse who is more than 10 years younger than you. Thus, if you select your teenage niece or cousin as your designated beneficiary, you must disregard their actual age and treat them as 10 years younger than yourself when determining your required minimum distributions.

Although you cannot avoid this 10-year differential rule when computing the required minimum distributions during your lifetime, the rule does not apply to your designated beneficiary after your death. By planning ahead, as discussed in this chapter, you can simplify the required minimum distribution calculations for your designated beneficiary.

If you are married, you must generally obtain the consent of your spouse to designate any other person as the designated beneficiary of your qualified plan account. Spousal consent is currently not required under federal law if an IRA is involved.

Selecting a Younger Beneficiary:

The following questions and answers will explain how to figure your required minimum distributions if your designated beneficiary as of your required beginning date is not your spouse, and is more than 10 years younger than you are. Special rules apply in spousal IRA rollover situations. See Question 3.18.

Question 4.1: *Roberta Smart has an IRA at the EFG Bank. She will be age 70 on June 1, 1997 and age 70¹/₂ on December 1, 1997. Her son, Jason Smart, the designated beneficiary of her IRA, will be age 40 on August 1, 1997. What is the first year for which Roberta is required to receive a required minimum distribution from her IRA?*

Answer: The first year for which Roberta must receive a required minimum distribution from her IRA is called the "first distribution calendar year." For Roberta, this is the calendar year 1997, the year in which she attains age 70¹/₂.

Question 4.2: *Must Roberta receive a required minimum distribution from her IRA in the calendar year 1997?*

Answer: No. Although the first required minimum distribution is for the year 1997, Roberta has until her required beginning date to receive it.

Question 4.3: *What is Roberta's required beginning date?*

Answer: Roberta's required beginning date is April 1, 1998. The required beginning date for Roberta is April 1 of the calendar year following the calendar year in which she attains age 70¹/₂. Roberta attains age 70¹/₂ in the calendar year 1997. Her required beginning date is therefore April 1, 1998. This is the deadline for receiving the first required minimum distribution.

Roberta may receive the distribution for her first distribution calendar year at any time during the period commencing January 1, 1997 and ending April 1, 1998. Her projected tax position for each year should dictate when she should receive this distribution. The distribution will be taxable to Roberta in whichever year she receives it.

Question 4.4: *When must Roberta receive her required minimum distribution for her second distribution calendar year 1998?*

Answer: Roberta must receive the required minimum distribution for the calendar year 1998 during the period January 1, 1998 to December 31, 1998.

If Roberta delayed receipt of the first required minimum distribution for 1997 until April 1, 1998 (April, 1, 1998 is the required beginning date), she will have to report that distribution as well as the required minimum distribution for 1998 in her 1998 income tax return.

Question 4.5: *Assume that Roberta timely selected her son, Jason, as the designated beneficiary of her IRA. Roberta would like to receive her required minimum distribution for her first distribution calendar year 1997 during 1997. Roberta's IRA account balance as of December*

31, 1996 is $100,000. Would you please determine Roberta's required minimum distribution for her first distribution calendar year 1997?

Answer: Roberta's required minimum distribution for 1997 is $3,816.79. This is determined as follows:

Roberta's IRA account balance as of December 31, 1996 (account balance as of the end of the preceding year is used)	$ 100,000
Divided by the applicable divisor for the calendar year 1997 which is 26.2 years	÷26.2 years
Required minimum distribution for the calendar year 1997	$3,816.79

To avoid an IRS penalty Roberta must receive at least $3,816.79 from her IRA by her required beginning date of April 1, 1998. She may of course withdraw more than that.

Question 4.6: *The joint life expectancy of Roberta and Jason is greater than 26.2 years. Why did you divide the account balance by only 26.2 years?*

Answer: The IRS has a special rule that applies in calculating the IRA owner's lifetime required minimum distributions if the nonspouse designated beneficiary is more than 10 years younger than the owner.

The special 10-year differential rule is called the Minimum Distribution Incidental Benefit Requirement (MDIB).

A special IRS "applicable divisor table" is used to compute the required minimum distributions that Roberta must receive under the MDIB requirement. Roberta must determine her attained age as of her birthday in the calendar year that she is age $70\frac{1}{2}$. Roberta is age 70 on June 1, 1997 and attains age $70\frac{1}{2}$ on December 1, 1997. Roberta therefore is age 70 in her first distribution calendar year 1997. Jason is age 40 in the calendar year 1997.

The IRS table assumes that Jason is 10 years younger than Roberta in order to determine Roberta's required minimum distributions. According to the IRS table, when Roberta is age 70, Jason is tentatively deemed to be age 60. The applicable divisor table is shown in the Appendix as "Table for Determining Applicable Divisor for MDIB."

If you wish to check the factor of 26.2, look up the joint life expectancy table found in Table II of IRS Publication 590, which is reproduced in the Appendix of this book. A joint life expectancy of a 70- and a 60-year-old is 26.2 years. The joint life expectancy can also be found in Table VI of 1.72-9 of the Income Tax Regulations.

Question 4.7: *Does this special rule regarding the applicable divisor table also apply to required minimum distributions from qualified company plans and other retirement savings arrangements such as 403(b) annuity contracts and self-employed Keogh or SEP accounts?*

Answer: Yes. This special rule applies to all retirement savings arrangements that are subject to the required minimum distribution rules.

Question 4.8: *Assume that an IRA owner is married and selects his spouse as his designated beneficiary. Further assume that his spouse is 15 years younger than the IRA owner. Must the IRA owner use the applicable divisor table in determining his required minimum distributions during his lifetime?*

Answer: No. The applicable divisor table is not used if the IRA owner timely selects his spouse as his designated beneficiary. The joint life expectancy of both the IRA owner and his spouse under the IRS tables is used in determining the IRA owner's required minimum distributions. See Chapter 3.

Question 4.9: *Assume that an IRA owner is married and selects his spouse as his designated beneficiary. Further assume that his spouse is five years younger than the IRA owner. May the IRA owner use the applicable divisor table in determining his required minimum distributions during his lifetime?*

Answer: No. The applicable divisor table can never be used if the IRA owner timely selects his spouse as his designated beneficiary. If the spouse is only five years younger than the IRA owner, she cannot be treated as if 10 years younger than the IRA owner by improperly using the applicable divisor table. The joint life expectancy of the IRA owner and his spouse under the IRS tables is used in determining the IRA owner's required minimum distributions whenever the spouse is the designated beneficiary. See Chapter 3.

Question 4.10: *Would you please indicate the applicable divisor that Roberta must use in determining her required minimum distributions for each distribution calendar year from 1997 through 2007, assuming Jason was timely selected as her designated beneficiary?*

Answer: The following schedule lists the applicable divisor that Roberta must use in determining her required minimum distributions for each distribution calendar year.

Roberta's Age	Calendar Year	Distribution Year	Applicable Divisor
70	1997	1	26.2
71	1998	2	25.3
72	1999	3	24.4
73	2000	4	23.5
74	2001	5	22.7
75	2002	6	21.8
76	2003	7	20.9
77	2004	8	20.1
78	2005	9	19.2
79	2006	10	18.4
80	2007	11	17.6

A complete copy of this table is found in IRS Publication 590, "Appendix E." The table is reproduced in the Appendix of this book and is called "Table for Determining Applicable Divisor for MDIB."

Question 4.11: *Would you please tell me why the factor of 25.3 years is used in order to determine Roberta's required minimum distribution for her second distribution calendar-year 1998?*

Answer: The IRS applicable divisor table must be used since the designated beneficiary of Roberta's IRA is Jason, and Jason is more than 10 years younger than Roberta. In the year 1998, Roberta is age 71, and Jason is tentatively deemed to be age 61. The joint life expectancy for a 71- and 61-year-old under the IRS tables is 25.3 years. The applicable divisor table reflects this by providing an applicable divisor of 25.3 for a 71-year-old account owner.

Question 4.12: *Assume that Roberta did not select Jason as her designated beneficiary until April 30, 1998. Also assume that Roberta did not select a designated beneficiary prior to that date. Would the MDIB requirement be applicable to Roberta?*

Answer: No. The MDIB requirement is not applicable unless a person who is more than 10 years younger than the account owner is selected as Roberta's designated beneficiary by no later than Roberta's required beginning date of April 1, 1998. If a designated beneficiary has not been selected by the required beginning date, then Roberta must figure her required minimum distributions using only her own life expectancy, as illustrated in the next question.

Question 4.13: *Assume that Roberta did not select a designated beneficiary of her IRA as of her required beginning date of April 1, 1998. How much must Roberta receive as a required minimum distribution for her first distribution calendar year 1997?*

Answer: Roberta must use a single life expectancy from Table V of section 1.72-9 of the Income Tax Regulations. This table, called Table I in IRS Publication 590, is reproduced in the Appendix of this book. Roberta's life expectancy for her first distribution year of 1997 is based upon her attained age as of her birthday in the year she attains age $70^1/_2$. In 1997, when she reached age $70^1/_2$, Roberta had her 70th birthday. Looking up the life expectancy for a 70-year-old in the IRS table gives a single life expectancy of 16 years. The required minimum distribution for her first distribution calendar year 1997 is $6,250. This amount is determined as follows:

Roberta's IRA account balance as of December 31, 1996 (the end of the year preceding the 1997 distribution year)	$100,000
Divided by the single life expectancy of Roberta for the calendar year 1997 which is 16 years	÷16 years
Required minimum distribution for the calendar year 1997	$6,250.00

Question 4.14: *Assume that the MDIB requirement was not part of the IRS rules. What is the true joint life expectancy of Roberta and Jason in the calendar year 1997?*

Answer: The joint life expectancy of a 70- and a 40-year-old is 42.9 years according to the IRS joint life expectancy tables; see Table II from IRS Publication 590, which is reproduced in the Appendix of the book.

Question 4.15: *If Roberta were not subject to the 10-year differential MDIB rule, she could have elected to calculate her required minimum distributions for years after the first distribution year under the term-certain method. How does the life expectancy period she must use under the MDIB requirement differ from the amount allowed by the term-certain method?*

Answer: The following schedule compares the term-certain method against the applicable divisor that must be used under the MDIB rule for Roberta's first five distribution years. Roberta must use the lesser of the applicable divisor or term-certain period during her lifetime.

For example, on their birthdays in 1997, the year Roberta attains age 70^1/$_2$, Roberta and Jason are age 70 and 40, respectively. For the first distribution year 1997, Roberta must use the applicable divisor that assumes that Jason is 10 years younger than she is. Thus, the applicable divisor of 26.2 years is based on the joint expectancy of a 70-year-old and 60-year-old. If the MDIB rule did not apply, the joint life expectancy of 42.9 years based upon their actual ages of 70 and 40 would be used for 1997, and decreased by one for each subsequent year.

Roberta's Age	Calendar Year	Distribution Year	Applicable Divisor	Term-Certain Method	Period Used During Roberta's Lifetime
70	1997	1	26.2	42.9	26.2
71	1998	2	25.3	41.9	25.3
72	1999	3	24.4	40.9	24.4
73	2000	4	23.5	39.9	23.5
74	2001	5	22.7	38.9	22.7
75	2002	6	21.8	37.9	21.8

Question 4.16: *The applicable divisor table changes by less than one for each distribution calendar year. Is it proper to refer to the applicable divisor as a recalculation method?*

Answer: No. Although the applicable divisor table operates like the recalculation method discussed in Chapter 3, it is not a recalculation method under the IRS rules. The applicable divisor table is not a method but merely a special table that is based upon a maximum age spread of 10 years between the IRA owner and a nonspouse designated beneficiary.

Distributions to Designated Beneficiary Following IRA Owner's Death:

The following questions and answers will guide you through the special distribution rules that apply to a designated beneficiary when an IRA owner who is more than 10 years older dies on or after the required beginning date.

Question 4.17: *Does the MDIB requirement apply after the death of the IRA owner?*

Answer: No. According to the IRS proposed regulations and IRS Publication 590, the MDIB requirement does not apply in years after the death of the IRA owner.

Question 4.18: *Assume that Roberta timely selected Jason as her designated beneficiary and timely elected the term-certain method. Also assume that Roberta dies in the calendar year 2002 after receiving her required minimum distribution for the distribution calendar year 2002. If Jason survives Roberta, when will he have to start to receive his required minimum distributions from Roberta's IRA?*

Answer: Jason must start to receive his required minimum distributions from Roberta's IRA during the calendar year following Roberta's death. The calendar year following Roberta's death is the calendar year 2003.

Question 4.19: *What is the true joint life expectancy of Roberta and Jason in the year Roberta attained age 70 ¹/₂?*

Answer: Roberta attained age 70 ¹/₂ in 1997. In that year she is age 70 and Jason is age 40. The joint life expectancy of a 70- and 40-year-old under the IRS tables is 42.9 years.

Question 4.20: *Over what period of time may Jason receive his required minimum distributions from Roberta's IRA?*

Answer: Jason must commence distributions from Roberta's IRA in the calendar year 2003, the year after the year of Roberta's death. Jason may use a life expectancy period of 36.9 years in determining his required minimum distributions.

Question 4.21: *How did you determine the 36.9-year life expectancy period that Jason may use after Roberta's death?*

Answer: Roberta timely selected Jason as her designated beneficiary and timely elected the term-certain method. The term-certain period as of Roberta's required beginning date is 42.9 years (see Question 4.19). Since Roberta lived for six distribution calendar years, the remaining period that is left in the 42.9-year period is 36.9 years. That period of time is available for Jason. This is true although Roberta, while she was alive, could not use the 42.9-year period because of the MDIB rule discussed earlier this chapter.

Question 4.22: *How should Roberta elect the term-certain method?*

Answer: Roberta should elect in writing with the IRA institution by certified mail, return receipt requested, that she wishes to use the term-certain method and not the recalculation method. She should make the election by her required beginning date April 1, 1998.

Question 4.23: *Could Roberta use the recalculation method of figuring life expectancy instead of the term-certain method?*

Answer: Yes. However the recalculation method can only be used for Roberta and not for Jason. Under the recalculation method, Roberta would use her age as of her birthday in each year for purposes of looking up joint life expectancy in the IRS tables. However, this is academic since the MDIB rule must be used during Roberta's lifetime.

Question 4.24 *Can the recalculation method ever be used for Jason?*

Answer: No. The recalculation method may never be used for a nonspouse designated beneficiary. During Roberta's lifetime, Jason's life expectancy must be reduced by one each year under the hybrid method discussed later in this chapter.

Question 4.25: *If Roberta does not timely elect the term-certain method, what happens?*

Answer: Many IRA plan documents automatically default into the recalculation method where the term-certain method is not timely elected. The default would require that Roberta's life expectancy must be recalculated for purposes of figuring the required minimum distributions that she must receive during her lifetime. However, since Jason's life expectancy may not be recalculated, Roberta would have to use the hybrid method to figure her joint life expectancy with Jason. However, this is academic since the MDIB rule must be used during Roberta's lifetime.

Question 4.26: *Roberta is concerned that after her death, Jason may be confused about the IRA distribution period that he may use. Roberta would like to make a specific term-certain election in order to clarify the IRA distribution period for Jason. Can you suggest any language that Roberta could use in her term-certain election?*

Answer: Roberta should file a term-certain election with the IRA institution by certified mail, return receipt requested. The election may state something like this:

> I, Roberta Smart, have timely designated my son, Jason Smart, as my designated beneficiary. I hereby elect that my required minimum distributions to me be based upon a term-certain period of 42.9 years based upon my life expectancy and my designated beneficiary's life expectancy determined in the calendar year 1997. The calendar year 1997 is the calendar year in which I attained age $70^1/_2$. However, I recognize that during my lifetime the required minimum distributions to me shall be based upon the Minimum Distribution Incidental Benefit Requirement and this requires the use of a special applicable divisor table in order to determine my required minimum distributions. However, in the calendar year following my death and for all calendar years thereafter my son, Jason, may use the original 42.9-year term-certain period reduced by one for each distribution calendar year that I was alive in order to determine the required minimum distributions that he must receive from this IRA after my death. The year of my death shall count as a full year in this computation. In addition, Jason after my death shall be permitted to accelerate distributions from time to time.

The above election is illustrative only. It should be reviewed by a professional advisor and modified to the extent necessary. It must of course be signed and dated by Roberta Smart.

Question 4.27: *Why should Roberta or any other IRA account owner prepare such a detailed election as described above?*

Answer: If the election is detailed, then it provides a guidepost for the IRA institution and Jason. Upon Roberta's death in the calendar year 2002, Jason automatically knows that he may receive his required minimum distributions from Roberta's IRA over a period that does not exceed 36.9 years. The 42.9-year period is reduced by six years.

Question 4.28: *If Jason survives Roberta and then dies, who receives the remaining payments from Roberta's IRA?*

Answer: Jason's estate.

Question 4.29: *What options are available to Jason's estate?*

Answer: Distributions should be paid to the estate over the remaining term-certain period left unused at Jason's death. Jason's executor may accelerate in whole or in part the remaining required minimum distributions of Roberta's IRA. In addition, Jason's executor may assign the rights to the remaining required minimum distributions to Jason's heirs. Jason's heirs may then receive the remaining required minimum distributions from Roberta's IRA or accelerate the distributions from Roberta's IRA from time to time.

Question 4.30: *Assume that Roberta does not wish to make a detailed election with the IRA institution but still wants to use the term-certain method so that Jason may use it in the years after her death. What should Roberta do?*

Answer: She may write to the IRA institution and state that she wishes to use the term-certain method. This should automatically trigger the same results that was previously described in Questions 4.26 through 4.29. The only difference is that Jason and the IRA institution do not have a specific road map as to the integration of the Minimum Distribution Incidental Benefit Requirement (MDIB) and the required minimum distribution rules.

Question 4.31: *Assume that Roberta timely made the specific term-certain election and died during the calendar year 2002 after receiving her required minimum distribution from her IRA* *for the calendar year 2002. Assume that the balance in Roberta's IRA as of December 31, 2002 is $115,000. Would you please calculate Jason's required minimum distribution for the calendar year 2003?*

Answer: Jason must commence his required minimum distributions from Roberta's IRA in the calendar year 2003. In the calendar year following Roberta's death and all years thereafter, Jason may use the balance that is left in the original term-certain period of 42.9 years after subtracting the six distribution calendar years that have elapsed for the calendar year 1997 through 2002. Therefore Jason has a remaining life expectancy period of 36.9 years that he may use in determining his required minimum distributions from Roberta's IRA. Jason's required minimum distribution for the calendar year 2003 is $3,116.53.

This is determined as follows:

Roberta's IRA account balance as of December 31, 2002	$115,000.00
Divided by the life expectancy available to Jason for the calendar year 2003 which is 36.9 years	÷36.9 years
Jason's required minimum distribution for the calendar year 2003	$3,116.53

Question 4.32: *Assume the facts in Question 4.31. Also assume that Roberta's IRA account balance as of December 31, 2003 is $118,000. Would you please calculate Jason's required minimum distribution for the calendar year 2004 under the term-certain method?*

Answer: Jason's required minimum distribution for the calendar year 2004 under the term-certain method is $3,286.91.

This is determined as follows:

Roberta's IRA account balance as of December 31, 2003	$118,000.00
Divided by the remaining life expectancy available to Jason under the term-certain method for the calendar year 2004 which is 35.9 years	÷35.9 years
Required minimum distribution for the calendar year 2004	$3,286.91

Question 4.33: *Assume the facts in Question 4.31. Would you please indicate the life expectancy under the term-certain method that Jason may use in determining his required minimum distributions from Roberta's IRA for the calendar years 2003 through 2007?*

Answer: The following schedule indicates the life expectancy that Jason may use under the term-certain method in determining his required minimum distributions for the calendar years 2003 through 2007.

Jason's Age	Calendar Year	Term-certain Life Expectancy
46	2003	36.9
47	2004	35.9
48	2005	34.9
49	2006	33.9
50	2007	32.9

As you can see the life expectancy that can be used by Jason drops by one for each calendar year.

Question 4.34: *Assume that Roberta timely selects Jason as the designated beneficiary of her IRA. Under the terms of the IRA plan, the default option is the recalculation method if the term-certain method is not elected. In determining Roberta's required minimum distributions during her lifetime, does it make a difference to her whether or not she timely elected the term-certain method or defaulted into the recalculation method?*

Answer: No. Since Jason is more than 10 years younger than Roberta, then during Roberta's lifetime, the Minimum Distribution Incidental Benefit Requirement is applicable. Roberta must therefore use the applicable divisor table in calculating her required minimum distributions during her lifetime. The applicable divisor is based upon a 10-year age difference between Roberta and Jason for each year that Roberta is alive. The IRS requires that Roberta's required minimum distribution from her IRA be determined by dividing her IRA account balance as of the appropriate December 31 date by the lesser of (1) the applicable divisor or (2) the applicable life expectancy determined under the term-certain method or the hybrid method. Naturally, the applicable divisor table is used while Roberta is alive. The applicable life expectancy would never be used while Roberta is alive, since the actual age difference between Roberta and Jason is 30 years. The life expectancy method, whether it be term-certain or the hybrid method, cannot be used because it would always result in a greater period than that determined under the applicable divisor table.

Question 4.35: *If Roberta failed to make a term-certain election and defaulted into the recalculation method with respect to her own life expectancy, how does this affect the minimum distributions that Jason must receive from her IRA in calendar years after her death?*

Answer: Upon Roberta's death, Jason must use the hybrid method to determine his single life expectancy. This method uses the IRS single life expectancy table for Jason as of the calendar year that Roberta attained age 70½ and reduces that life expectancy by one for each subsequent year that Roberta was alive. The reduction by one is also applicable for the calendar year in which Roberta died. Jason's life expectancy under the IRS single life expectancy table is determined under Table V of 1.72-9 of the Income Tax Regulations. This table, called Table I in IRS Publication 590 is shown in the Appendix of this book.

Question 4.36: *How would Jason determine his required minimum distributions under the hybrid method if Roberta died in 2002 after receiving her required minimum distribution for that year?*

Answer: Under the hybrid method, Jason must first determine his single life expectancy in 1997, Roberta's first distribution year. Under the single life expectancy table shown in the Appendix, the life expectancy of Jason in the calendar year 1997 at age 40 is 42.5 years. Jason then subtracts the six distribution calendar years through 2002 that Roberta was alive. Therefore, for 2003, Jason has a remaining life expectancy under the hybrid method of 36.5 years that he may use in determining his required minimum distributions from Roberta's IRA. The following schedule indicates the life expectancy that Jason may use under the hybrid method in determining his required minimum distributions for the calendar years 2003 through 2007. As you can see, the life expectancy used for 2003, the year following the year of Roberta's death, is reduced by one for each subsequent year.

Jason's Age	Calendar Year	Hybrid Method Life Expectancy
46	2003	36.5
47	2004	35.5
48	2005	34.5
49	2006	33.5
50	2007	32.5

To calculate the required minimum distribution for each year, Jason would divide the hybrid method life expectancy into the account balance of the IRA as of the end of the preceding year. If for example, the account balance as of December 31, 2003, was $122,000, Jason would have to receive at least $3,436.62 from the IRA ($122,000 divided by 35.5) during 2004 to satisfy the required minimum distribution rules.

Question 4.37: *Is the difference between the hybrid method and the term-certain method significant as far as Jason is concerned?*

Answer: No. Jason's life expectancy is practically identical under both methods. The following schedule compares the two methods for the calendar year 2003 through 2007.

Jason's Age	Calendar Year	Term-certain Life Expectancy	Hybrid Method Life Expectancy
46	2003	36.9	36.5
47	2004	35.9	35.5
48	2005	34.9	34.5
49	2006	33.9	33.5
50	2007	32.9	32.5

Question 4.38: *Under the hybrid method, why isn't Roberta's life expectancy considered in the calculation for the calendar year 2003 and thereafter?*

Answer: Roberta has a zero life expectancy under the recalculation method in the calendar year following her year of death and all years thereafter. Since Roberta died in the calendar year 2002, she has a zero life expectancy in the calendar year 2003 and all subsequent years.

Question 4.39: *Assume that Roberta timely selects Jason as the designated beneficiary of her IRA and timely elects the term-certain method, and she dies during the calendar year 2002 before receiving her required minimum distribution for the calendar year 2002. What should Jason do in order to avoid any possible 50% penalty with the Internal Revenue Service?*

Answer: Jason should determine the amount of the required minimum distribution that Roberta should have received for the calendar year 2002. Jason should then receive the amount calculated as Roberta's required minimum distribution for the calendar year 2002 as soon as possible. The IRS will not assert any penalty if Jason acts promptly. In addition, Jason must commence his required minimum distributions from Roberta's IRA in the calendar year 2003 and in all calendar years thereafter.

CHAPTER 5

Using a Custodial Account or Irrevocable Trust for a Designated Beneficiary Who Is a Minor

When the beneficiary of a qualified plan or IRA is a very young child, it may be better to have the distributions paid to a Custodian who will receive the distributions on behalf of the minor, rather than to the child directly.

Another alternative is to use an irrevocable trust when your intended designated beneficiary is a minor.

This chapter will discuss how a custodial account or irrevocable trust can be used to handle retirement death benefits for the benefit of a minor.

Benefits of a Custodial Account:

The following series of questions and answers explain how a custodial account can be used to receive qualified plan or IRA benefits.

Question 5.1: *Is there any way for an IRA distribution to be payable for the benefit of a minor after the death of the IRA owner while avoiding the jurisdiction of the local probate courts?*

Answer: Yes. Either a special irrevocable trust (discussed below in this chapter starting with Question 5.55) can be created to receive the IRA distributions on behalf of the minor or, if permitted under state law, a Custodian under the Uniform Gifts to Minors Act or Uniform Transfers to Minors Act can be designated to receive the IRA distributions on behalf of the minor. In the event that the IRA owner dies before his required beginning date, then the Trustee of the irrevocable trust may make the appropriate timely written election of a distribution method on behalf of the minor. A Custodian generally under state law does not have the authority to make any election on behalf of the minor. However, many IRA plan documents permit an IRA owner to select a distribution method on behalf of a designated beneficiary in the event the IRA owner dies before his required beginning date. If that option is available to the IRA owner, then the IRA owner who is selecting a Custodian for the benefit of a minor as a beneficiary may make a protective election of a distribution method in the event that he dies before his required beginning date. The protective election is discussed in this chapter. The rules that are triggered in the event the IRA owner dies on or after his required beginning date were previously discussed in detail in Chapter 4.

Question 5.2: *How do you know if a Custodian can receive IRA distributions?*

Answer: The Uniform Gifts to Minors Act or Uniform Transfers to Minors Act for the particular state will generally have specific provisions in the statute that permits the Custodian to receive retirement type distributions on behalf of the minor.

Question 5.3: *What type of language should one look for in order to determine whether or not the particular state permits retirement assets to be paid to a Custodian?*

Answer: Many states (e.g., Alabama, Colorado, Florida, Massachusetts, North Dakota, Rhode Island, and Virginia) use the following language in their Uniform Transfers to Minors Act:

> "A person having the right to designate the recipient of property upon the occurrence of a future event may revocably nominate a custodian to receive the property for a minor beneficiary . . . . The nomination may be made in a will, trust . . . or in a writing designating a beneficiary of contractual rights which is registered with or delivered to the payor, issuer or other obligor of the contractual rights."

The Uniform Gifts to Minors Act adopted in New York State, for example, permits gifts by beneficiary designation. The statute permits a Custodian to be the beneficiary of a pension, retirement, death benefit, deferred compensation, or other employee benefit plan.

Question 5.4: *If the beneficiary on behalf of the minor is a Custodian under the Uniform Gifts to Minors Act or Uniform Transfers to Minors Act, may the Custodian elect the distribution method for the IRA death benefits?*

Answer: No. Custodians under the Uniform Gifts to Minors Act or Uniform Transfers to Minors Act are not granted the same powers as a Trustee and have no right to elect a method of payment of the IRA death benefits. This, of course, could be changed by state legislation.

Question 5.5: *Why is it better to name a Custodian under the Uniform Gifts to Minors Act or Uniform Transfers to Minors Act on behalf of the minor as the beneficiary of the IRA death benefits instead of the minor directly?*

Answer: If the minor was named the direct beneficiary of IRA benefits, the local probate court could require that a guardian for the minor's property be appointed. Naming a

Custodian eliminates the jurisdiction of the local probate court. In addition, the Custodian under the Uniform Gifts to Minors Act or Uniform Transfers to Minors Act has a greater degree of flexibility in applying the funds for the use and benefit of the minor.

Question 5.6: *Who may be selected as the Custodian for the minor?*

Answer: State law determines who may be selected as the Custodian. Generally, the Custodian may be a member of the minor's family such as the minor's parent, grandparent, brother, sister, uncle, or aunt. Some states permit a trust company to act as Custodian, while other states permit any adult person to act as Custodian.

Question 5.7: *Should the donor ever be selected as a Custodian?*

Answer: No. According to the IRS and the federal courts if the Custodian is the donor and the custodial account is still in existence at the date of death of the donor, then the value of the property transferred to the custodial account is included in the gross estate of the donor for federal estate tax purposes.

Question 5.8: *If a grandparent during his lifetime made a gift of $1,000 to a custodial account for the benefit of a grandchild and named him- or herself as Custodian, what should he or she do?*

Answer: The grandparent should immediately resign as Custodian and the parent of the child or another member of the family should be made the Custodian.

Question 5.9: *A grandparent, Charles Smith, wishes to establish a custodial account in the amount of $5,000 for the benefit of his grandchild, Michael Smith. His son, George Smith, is selected as the Custodian. What should Charles do in order to establish the custodial account?*

Answer: The grandparent, Charles Smith, should make out a check for $5,000 payable to George Smith as Custodian under the Uniform Gifts to Minors Act of State X for the benefit of Michael Smith until his 18th birthday (or 21st birthday, depending on state law). George should then open up an account with a broker or other financial institution in the name of George Smith as Custodian under the Uniform Gifts to Minors Act of State X for the benefit of Michael Smith until his 18th birthday (or 21st birthday, depending on state law) and endorse the check over to the broker or other financial institution. If these steps are taken, then the $5,000 gift will never be included in the estate of the grandparent, Charles Smith, under any set of circumstances. In addition, the custodial account will not be included in the estate of George Smith as Custodian since George Smith's funds were not used to establish the custodial account.

Question 5.10: *If a grandparent lives in New York State and his or her grandchild lives in Florida, where should the custodial account be established?*

Answer: The custodial arrangement is governed by state law. Many states allow the Custodian to be appointed pursuant to the law of the state where the transferor resides, the state where the minor resides or the state where the Custodian resides. If the grandchild lives in Florida, then it is probably best that the custodian laws of the State of Florida be used since the Custodian would probably reside in Florida as well.

Question 5.11: *May the Custodian use the funds in the custodial account to support a minor?*

Answer: No. Several state courts have held that the Custodian may not legally use the custodial account in order to satisfy the support obligations of the parents. Thus, even if the Uniform Gifts to Minors Act statute seems to allow the Custodian to use the custodial account for the support and maintenance of the minor, the Custodian should not do so unless the parents do not have the ability to satisfy their support obligations to the minor. If the minor must be supported and the parents refuse to support the minor, then the Custodian should bring this to the attention of the state court and request permission to use the custodial funds for the support of the minor. The court may authorize such use or force the parents to prove that they have no assets. The custodial funds are assets of the child and may not be used to avoid the support obligation of the parents.

Question 5.12: *Why is there an issue as to whether the Custodian may use the custodial account for the support of the minor?*

Answer: Several states have language in their custodian statutes that state the following:

> "The custodian shall pay over to the minor for expenditure by him, or expend for the minor's benefit, so much or all of the custodial property as the custodian deems advisable for the support, maintenance, education and benefit of the minor in the manner, at the time and to the extent that the custodian in his discretion deems suitable and proper, with or without court order, with or without regard to the duty of himself or any other person to support the minor or his ability to do so . . ."

The above language causes the problem and the litigation because the Custodian thinks that the custodial funds can be used to take care of the support of the minor without considering the issue of the parental obligation of support.

The state courts have held that the Custodian may not use the custodial account for a support obligation of the parent. It makes no difference as to who may be the Custodian. In one case the minor child successfully sued the Custodian who happened to be the minor's mother.

Question 5.13: *How have some states avoided the confusing language described in the above question?*

Answer: A number of states have revised their custodian statutes to clearly eliminate the inference that the custodial funds may be used for support of the minor. These states have custodian statutes that state the following:

> "A custodian may deliver or pay to the minor or expend for the minor's benefit so much of the custodial property as the custodian considers advisable for the use and benefit of the minor, without court order and without regard to (1) the duty or ability of the custodian personally or of any other person to support the minor, or (2) any other income or property of the minor which may be applicable or available for that purpose.
>
> * * *
>
> A delivery, payment, or expenditure . . . is in addition to, not in substitution for, and does not affect any obligation of a person to support the minor."

Thus, these clarifying statutes should clearly deter the Custodian from using the custodial funds in order to satisfy the parental obligation to support the minor. Obviously the funds may have to be used to support the minor if the parents do not have the resources to support the minor.

Question 5.14: *Does the IRS always tax the income earned on the custodial account to the minor?*

Answer: No. If the Custodian uses the custodial funds to discharge the legal obligation of a parent to support or maintain a minor, then according to the IRS the parent is taxed on the income earned on the custodial property to the extent that the property is so used. The IRS will attempt to tax the parent on the income used to support the minor even if the parent is not the Custodian.

Question 5.15: *Is there a defense that can be used by the parent in order to avoid being taxed on custodial account income used to support the child?*

Answer: Yes. The defense is that the Custodian in the absence of a court order may not use the custodial funds to eliminate the parental obligation to support the minor. Therefore, the Custodian is obligated to return the funds to the custodial account and therefore the parent should not be required to pay taxes on the erroneous application of the funds by the Custodian. This defense is based upon case law and the custodian statutes that are applicable in many states. Many state statutes provide that an expenditure by a Custodian for the use and benefit of a minor does not affect any obligation of a person to support the minor.

Question 5.16: *A Custodian may expend funds for the use and benefit of the minor. What type of expenditures may the Custodian make on behalf of the minor?*

Answer: The Custodian may pay a minor's legally enforceable obligations such as tax liabilities or tort claims. If the parents were not affluent and could not afford to send the child to a private college, then it is possible that the Custodian could legally use the custodial funds to pay for college tuition.

Question 5.17: *What is considered to be a parent's support obligation to a child?*

Answer: A parent's support obligation to a child is the duty to provide the child with necessaries. Expenditures for a child's business use is not considered a necessary. Whether an expenditure is a necessary depends on the station in life of the parent and his or her ability to pay for the expenditure. Whether or not college tuition payments are a necessary is based upon state law. A state court might find that a wealthy parent who promised his or her son or daughter a college education is legally obligated to pay for the college tuition and expenses but a parent who earns a modest living does not have this obligation.

Owner Dies Before Required Beginning Date:

The following questions and answers illustrate the distribution rules that would apply if an IRA owner selects a Custodian as the beneficiary of the account and the owner dies before his or her required beginning date.

Question 5.18: *Jack Phillips, who is age 65 on June 1, 1995, has several IRA accounts. He is fond of his grandson, Craig Phillips, age four, and would like upon his death to have one of his IRA accounts used for the benefit of Craig. Jack is not in the best of health. Craig's father, Thomas Phillips, earns a reasonable salary. Thomas files a joint return with his wife, Mary, and they will be in the 31% federal income tax bracket for many years to come. Jack selects an IRA containing approximately $20,000 to be used for the benefit of his grandson, Craig. He would like to select a Custodian for the benefit of Craig as the beneficiary of his IRA accounts. How should the IRA beneficiary form read?*

Answer: The beneficiary of Jack Phillips' IRA should read something like this:

> Thomas Phillips, Custodian for Craig Phillips under the State X Uniform Gifts to Minors Act until the 18th birthday of Craig Phillips and then to Craig Phillips directly after he attains his 18th birthday.

The title should be based upon the state law where the IRA is located. In addition, some states allow you to use age 18 or age 21. If you feel that age 21 is a better age and the state law permits it, then use age 21. The social security number of Craig Phillips is used on the custodial account for income tax purposes.

Question 5.19: *If Jack Phillips selects his son Thomas, as Custodian for his grandson Craig, to be the beneficiary of his IRA, is Thomas or Craig the designated beneficiary for tax purposes?*

Answer: Obviously, Craig Phillips is the designated beneficiary. Thomas Phillips will merely hold the funds in the custodian account for the benefit of Craig Phillips. Under state law the true owner of the custodial account is the minor. The IRS in Revenue Ruling 59-357 discussed the Uniform Gifts to Minors Act and the Model Gifts of Securities to Minors Act and concluded that the minor is the true owner of the assets in the custodial account. Revenue Ruling 59-357 states in part the following:

> "Uniform laws have been adopted in many states to facilitate gifts to minors. Generally, these laws eliminate the usual requirement that a guardian be appointed or a trust set up when a minor is to be the donee of a gift. . . .The Uniform Gifts to Minors Act provides . . . that a bank, trust company, or any adult may act as custodian. When a gift is made pursuant to the model or uniform act the property vests absolutely in the minor."

Question 5.20: *If Jack dies at age 67 in 1997, what distribution options are available to Thomas, as Custodian for Craig?*

Answer: Jack's required beginning date is April of the calendar year following the calendar year in which he attains age $70^1/_2$. If Jack dies before that date, then either a five-year distribution period or a life expectancy distribution period applies. The plan document may specify which option applies, or the plan may permit the designated beneficiary to elect which method applies. However, Thomas, as Custodian, lacks the legal authority to elect a distribution method. If the IRA prototype document allows Jack as the IRA owner to make a distribution method election, he should do so.

If the IRA owner dies before his required begining date, then under the five-year rule, the entire account must be distributed by no later than December 31 of the fifth year following the year of the account owner's death.

Under the life expectancy rule, payments from the account may be made over the life expectancy of the designated beneficiary. In this case, Craig's life expectancy would be used.

Question 5.21: *Should Jack Phillips make a protective election out of the five-year rule if the beneficiary of his IRA is Thomas Phillips, the Custodian for Craig Phillips?*

Answer: Yes. Since his son, Thomas Phillips, as Custodian may not legally elect out of the five-year rule under current state law, then Jack Phillips must make the protective election out of the five-year rule if the life expectancy rule is desired. This is important since it is possible that Jack Phillips may die before his required beginning date.

Question 5.22: *Why is the election out of the five-year rule generally the better approach?*

Answer: The life expectancy method has greater flexibility and takes advantage of the longer payout period that is available to Craig based upon his life expectancy. The life expectancy method also takes advantage of Craig's lower income tax bracket. As shown in Question 5.23, it is possible that under the kiddie tax rules for children under age 14, Craig could incur a substantial federal income tax liability if the five-year rule were applicable. That problem can be avoided if Craig's grandfather, Jack, makes a protective election out of the five-year rule so that distributions after his death would be based on Craig's life expectancy.

Question 5.23: *Assume that Jack Phillips dies at age 67 in 1997. Craig Phillips is age 6 in 1997. What are the tax ramifications if the five-year rule is applicable?*

Answer: If Jack Phillips dies at age 67 in 1997, then under the five-year rule the entire IRA account would have to be paid to the Custodian by no later than December 31, 2002. Craig is age 11 in 2002. The Custodian would not be permitted to do any effective long-term tax planning and the entire account would be subject to income taxes in the calendar year 2002. The Custodian would have no legal right under state law to demand partial payments from the IRA during the five-year period. Because Craig is under age 14 at the end of the calendar year 2002, a substantial portion of the IRA account would be taxed at his parents' 31% federal income tax bracket under the so-called kiddie tax rules. See Question 5.18. Assume that in 2002 the decedent's IRA account is worth $32,000 when it is distributed to the Custodian. Also assume that the kiddie tax threshold for minors under age 14 in 2002 is $2,000. Investment income over $2,000 is taxed at Craig's parents' rate:

	Income Tax Bracket
1st $1,000 of income	0%
2nd $1,000 of income	15%
Next $30,000 of income at parents' tax bracket since Craig is under age 14 in the calendar year 2002	31%

The estimated federal income tax liability to Craig for the calendar year 2002 is as follows:

1st $1,000	$ -0-
2nd $1,000 at 15%	150.00
Next $30,000 at 31%	9,300.00
Total federal income tax liability	$9,450.00

Question 5.24: *If Craig was age nine instead of age six in 1997 and the five-year rule was applicable, then what would Craig's income tax liability be in the calendar year 2002?*

Answer: The federal income tax liability would be significantly different since Craig is age 14 in the calendar year 2002 and the kiddie tax is not applicable. Assume the following federal income tax brackets are applicable to a minor age 14 or over in 2002:

	Income Tax Bracket
1st $1,000 of income	0%
Next $29,000 of income	15%
Next $2,000 of income	28%

The estimated federal income tax liability to Craig for the calendar year 2002 is as follows:

1st $1,000	$ -0-
Next $29,000 at 15%	4,350.00
Next $2,000 at 28%	560.00
Total federal income tax liability	$4,910.00

Question 5.25: *Assume that Craig was age six in 1997. Also assume that Jack dies in 1997 at age 67 and his IRA as of December 31, 1997 was valued at $22,000. Why would Craig's federal income tax liability be reduced if Jack Phillips had filed a protective written election in which he elected out of the five-year rule?*

Answer: If Jack Phillips had elected out of the five-year rule and died in 1997 at age 67, then the required minimum distributions would be based upon the life expectancy of Craig Phillips in 1998, which is the calendar year following Jack's year of death. In 1998 Craig is age seven. According to the IRS life expectancy tables Craig's life expectancy in 1998 is 74.7 years. The required minimum distribution for 1998 is based upon the decedent's IRA account balance as of December 31, 1997. If Jack's IRA as of December 31, 1997 is worth $22,000, then a required minimum distribution of $294.51 must be made to the Custodian on behalf of Craig in the calendar year 1998. This is calculated as follows:

Jack's IRA account balance as of December 31, 1997	$22,000.00
Divided by Craig's life expectancy in 1998	÷ 74.7 years
Required minimum distribution for calendar year 1998	$294.51

The life expectancy method permits Craig to take advantage of the standard deduction and minimize his federal income tax liability. Craig's income tax liability depends on the amount of his other income.

Question 5.26: *Assume that Craig has no other income for the calendar year 1998. Is there any federal income tax liability that Craig is subject to for the calendar year 1998?*

Answer: No. Craig is entitled to a standard deduction of more than $294.51 and, therefore, will incur no federal income tax liability for the calendar year 1998.

Question 5.27: *If Jack dies in 1997 and his IRA account has a balance of $23,000 as of December 31, 1998, what is the required minimum distribution that must be paid to the Custodian on behalf of Craig for the calendar year 1999 based upon the life expectancy method discussed in Question 5.25?*

Answer: The Custodian must receive a required minimum distribution of $312.08 for the calendar year 1999. The required minimum distribution is based upon the decedent's account balance as of December 31, 1998 divided by Craig's remaining life expectancy of 73.7 years. Craig's remaining life expectancy is based upon his initial life expectancy determined in 1998 of 74.7 reduced by one for each year after 1998. This is calculated as follows:

Jack's IRA balance as of December 31, 1998	$23,000.00
Divided by Craig's remaining life expectancy in 1999	÷ 73.7 years
Required minimum distribution for calendar year 1999	$312.08

Question 5.28: *Assume that the required minimum distributions were paid to the Custodian for each calendar year including the calendar year in which Craig attained age 18. Why is this an effective income tax planning arrangement?*

Answer: The Custodian would receive a substantial amount of tax free income for a 12-year period. For the calendar years 1998 through 2009 (when Craig attains age 18) the Custodian should receive amounts below Craig's standard deduction. If we assume the required minimum distributions, plus the interest income earned on such amounts by the Custodian averaged $500 per year over the 12-year period, then in essence Craig will receive approximately $6,000 in tax-free income. This is an excellent way of building up a nest egg for Craig's future.

Question 5.29: *If Jack wants to make a protective election what should he do?*

Answer: Jack should examine the IRA plan document in order to determine whether it permits him to make an election out of the five-year rule. If the IRA plan document permits him to make an election, then Jack Phillips should make a protective election out of the five-year rule with the IRA institution. The protective election should be signed and dated by Jack and sent to the IRA institution by certified mail, return receipt requested.

Question 5.30: *How could Jack specifically write a protective election with the IRA institution in order to elect out of the five-year rule and into the life expectancy rule?*

Answer: Assuming that the IRA plan document permits an election out of the five-year rule, the election should state the following:

> In the event that I, Jack Phillips, should die prior to my required beginning date of April 1, 2001, and I am survived by my grandson, Craig Phillips, then I elect that the required minimum distributions of my IRA account maintained with the ABC institution, Account No. 10006 be paid based upon the life expectancy of my designated beneficiary, Craig Phillips, and that while Craig Phillips is under the age of 18 that the required minimum distributions be paid to Thomas Phillips as Custodian for Craig Phillips under the State X Uniform Gifts to Minors Act or similar act until the 18th birthday of Craig Phillips and thereafter directly to Craig Phillips after he attains his 18th birthday. Upon Craig Phillips reaching age 18, he may accelerate distributions from this IRA at any time or transfer this IRA directly in whole or in part to any other institution provided that the IRA is still maintained in my name. Craig Phillips may accelerate distributions from any transferee IRA at any time after reaching his 18th birthday. The Custodian shall notify the ABC institution each year as to the amount of the required minimum distribution that shall be paid to the Custodian each calendar year. The ABC institution shall have no liability in determining the amount of the required minimum distribution that shall be paid to the Custodian. The life expectancy of Craig in the event that I die prior to my required beginning date shall be based upon Craig's life expectancy under the appropriate IRS table and shall be based upon his life expectancy as determined in the calendar year after my death. The first required minimum distribution must be paid to the Custodian by no later than the December 31st of the calendar year following the year of my death. Subsequent distributions must be paid by December 31 of each calendar year thereafter.

Question 5.31: *What must the Custodian, Thomas Phillips, do when Craig attains age 18 in 2009?*

Answer: Thomas Phillips must turn over the balance in the custodial account to Craig Phillips in 2009 because the custodial account was only to last until Craig's 18th birthday.

Question 5.32: *If Jack Phillips is unhappy about the ability of Craig to accelerate distributions at age 18, what should he do?*

Answer: He could set up an irrevocable trust to receive the IRA funds on behalf of Craig. The irrevocable trust for the benefit of Craig can be structured in such a manner so that Craig does not have access to a substantial portion of the Jack Phillips, deceased IRA until his 25th birthday, 30th birthday, or a later age.

Question 5.33: *Has Jack Phillips maximized the benefits to Craig under federal income tax law by having the required minimum distributions payable to the Custodian?*

Answer: No. If we assume that Craig's federal standard deduction will generally be in excess of the required minimum distributions and his other income during the calendar years 1998 through 2009, then Jack Phillips has not maximized the federal income tax benefits that are available to Craig.

––––––––––––

Question 5.34: *Assume that Craig's standard deduction for the calendar year 1998 is $700. Is Jack guilty of poor tax planning?*

Answer: Yes. If we assume that Craig's standard deduction for the calendar year 1998 is $700, then in effect Craig could have received gross income of up to $700 instead of $294.51 (the required minimum distribution for 1998) without incurring any federal income tax liability.

––––––––––––

Question 5.35: *How could Jack Phillips take advantage of Craig's federal standard deduction in making the protective election?*

Answer: Jack Phillips, together with his professional advisor, should estimate the amount of the federal standard deduction that will be available to Craig and integrate that estimate into the protective election. Craig's projected other income and state income taxes should be considered as well where applicable.

For example, assume that Jack Phillips and his professional advisor do not know what the federal standard deduction will be for Craig in the future. They estimate that it will be in the range of $700 to $1,000 over the next 15 years. Jack Phillips may use certain language in the protective election that may reduce Craig's overall income tax liability during the period of his minority. The protective election described in the answer to Question 5.30 could state "that the greater of the required minimum distribution or $1,000 shall be paid annually to Thomas Phillips, as Custodian . . ."

––––––––––––

Question 5.36: *What is the advantage of using the protective election language suggested in the answer to Question 5.35?*

Answer: By Jack Phillips's stating in the protective election "that the greater of the required minimum distribution or $1,000 shall be paid annually to Thomas Phillips, as Custodian . . .," he and his professional advisor have accomplished effective tax planning by maximizing use of Craig's standard deduction. If the average standard deduction over the 12-year period is $800, then in effect Craig will receive $9,600 in tax-free income.

––––––––––––

Question 5.37: *Assume that Jack Phillips dies in 1997 and Thomas Phillips, as Custodian for Craig, receives $1,000 in 1998 from Jack's IRA. Craig is age seven in 1998. If Craig has no other income, and his standard deduction in 1998 is $700, what is Craig's federal income tax liability for 1998?*

Answer: Craig's federal income tax liability in 1998 is $45.00. This is computed as follows:

Craig's gross income	$ 1,000.00
Less: Standard deduction	700.00
Taxable income	$ 300.00
Tax rate on 1st $700 of taxable income	15%
Federal income tax	$ 45.00

Craig's effective federal income tax rate is 4.5% ($45 ÷ $1,000). The income that is received by Thomas Phillips, as Custodian, is taxed to Craig at Craig's income tax rates.

Question 5.38: *Assume the same facts as in Question 5.35, and that in 1999, Thomas Phillips, as Custodian for Craig, receives $70 of interest income in addition to the $1,000 from Jack's IRA. What is Craig's federal income tax liability in 1999 if we assume that Craig's federal standard deduction in 1999 is $700?*

Answer: Craig's federal income tax liability in 1999 would be $55.50. This is computed as follows:

Craig's gross income	$ 1,070.00
Less: Standard deduction	700.00
Taxable income	$ 370.00
Tax rate on 1st $700 of taxable income	15%
Federal income tax$	55.50

Craig's effective federal income tax rate is 5.19% ($55.50 ÷ $1,070.00).

Question 5.39: *Assume that Jack Phillips made a timely protective election to avoid the five-year rule. Thomas Phillips, as Custodian for Craig, receives $1,000 annually from the Jack Phillips, deceased, IRA for each calendar year beginning with 1998 (the year following the year of Jack's death Craig attains his seventh birthday). Assume further that Jack's IRA earns a 7% interest rate and that the $1,000 distribution to Thomas Phillips, as Custodian, is made at the end of each calendar year. How much is left in Jack's IRA as of the end of calendar year 2009, the year in which Craig attains age 18?*

Answer: $31,659.76. The details of this computation are as follows:

Craig's Age	Year	Earnings	Actual Distribution	IRA Balance
	1997			$ 22,000.00
7	1998	1,540.00	1,000.00	22,540.00
8	1999	1,577.80	1,000.00	23,117.80
9	2000	1,618.25	1,000.00	23,736.05
10	2001	1,661.52	1,000.00	24,397.57
11	2002	1,707.83	1,000.00	25,105.40
12	2003	1,757.38	1,000.00	25,862.78
13	2004	1,810.39	1,000.00	26,673.17
14	2005	1,867.12	1,000.00	27,540.29
15	2006	1,927.82	1,000.00	28,468.11
16	2007	1,992.77	1,000.00	29,460.88
17	2008	2,062.26	1,000.00	30,523.14
18	2009	2,136.62	1,000.00	31,659.76
		$21,659.76	$12,000.00	

Question 5.40: *Assume that Thomas Phillips, as Custodian, earns a total of $5,500 on the annual distributions of $1,000 that he receives during the 12-year period. How much has Thomas Phillips, as Custodian for Craig, accumulated by the end of the calendar year 2009?*

Answer: Thomas Phillips, as Custodian for Craig Phillips, has accumulated approximately $17,500. This is computed as follows:

Distributions received from Jack Phillips' IRA during the period 1998 to 2009	$12,000.00
Earnings by the Custodian during the 12-year period	5,500.00*
Total	$17,500.00

*Federal income tax will be due on the distributions of $12,000 paid to the Custodian, plus the $5,500 of earnings realized by the Custodian. Assume that the taxes are paid by Craig's parents, and are estimated to be approximately $1,200. If the Custodian had paid these taxes through the custodian account, then the earnings by the Custodian would be reduced, and so would the taxes on the earnings.

Question 5.41: *At the end of calendar year 2009, to how much money does Craig have access?*

Answer: Craig will receive approximately $17,500 from the Custodian, plus he has the ability to draw $31,659.76 from the Jack Phillips, deceased, IRA. If Craig draws down the $31,659.76 from the Jack Phillips, deceased, IRA in one calendar year, then he will pay federal and state income taxes on that amount. Craig, therefore, has access to $49,159.76 ($17,500 + $31,659). The $17,500 is after tax monies and the $31,659 is before tax monies. If we assume that the $31,659 after deductions and his exemption is subject to an overall tax liability of approximately $5,000, then Craig will have access to a net amount of approximately $44,000.

Question 5.42: *Assume that only the required minimum distributions are paid to Craig's Custodian before Craig attains age 18 and thereafter to Craig based upon his life expectancy under the IRS tables. Further assume that the IRA earns 7% during the payout period. How much will Craig receive from the IRA over his life expectancy?*

Answer: As of 1998, the year following Jack's death, Craig's life expectancy, at age seven, is 74 years (74.7 rounded down to 74 for illustrative purposes). Craig will receive required minimum distributions of $731,908.09 based upon a 74-year life expectancy and assumed interest of 7% on $22,000, the balance of Jack's IRA as of December 31, 1997. This assumes that Craig does not accelerate distributions from the IRA during the payout period. The compounding effect of the interest is the key in this calculation. The following schedule illustrates the details of this calculation.

Initial amount: $22,000.00, Earnings: 7%

Distributions over 74 years

Year	Earnings	Required Minimum Distribution	Balance
			22,000.00
1	1,540.00	297.30	23,242.70
2	1,626.99	318.39	24,551.30
3	1,718.59	340.99	25,928.90
4	1,815.02	365.20	27,378.72
5	1,916.51	391.12	28,904.11
6	2,023.29	418.90	30,508.50
7	2,135.60	448.65	32,195.45
8	2,253.68	480.53	33,968.60
9	2,377.80	514.68	35,831.72
10	2,508.22	551.26	37,788.68
11	2,645.21	590.45	39,843.44
12	2,789.04	632.44	42,000.04
13	2,940.00	677.42	44,262.62
14	3,098.38	725.62	46,635.38
15	3,264.48	777.26	49,122.60
16	3,438.58	832.59	51,728.59
17	3,621.00	891.87	54,457.72

cont'd

(continued from previous page)

Year	Earnings	Required Minimum Distribution	Balance
18	3,812.04	955.40	57,314.36
19	4,012.01	1,023.47	60,302.90
20	4,221.20	1,096.42	63,427.68
21	4,439.94	1,174.59	66,693.03
22	4,668.51	1,258.36	70,103.18
23	4,907.22	1,348.14	73,662.26
24	5,156.36	1,444.36	77,374.26
25	5,416.20	1,547.49	81,242.97
26	5,687.01	1,658.02	85,271.96
27	5,969.04	1,776.50	89,464.50
28	6,262.52	1,903.50	93,823.52
29	6,567.65	2,039.64	98,351.53
30	6,884.61	2,185.59	103,050.55
31	7,213.54	2,342.06	107,922.03
32	7,554.54	2,509.81	112,966.76
33	7,907.67	2,689.68	118,184.75
34	8,272.93	2,882.55	123,575.13
35	8,650.26	3,089.38	129,136.01
36	9,039.52	3,311.18	134,864.35
37	9,440.50	3,549.06	140,755.79
38	9,852.91	3,804.21	146,804.49
39	10,276.31	4,077.90	153,002.90
40	10,710.20	4,371.51	159,341.59
41	11,153.91	4,686.52	165,808.98
42	11,606.63	5,024.51	172,391.10
43	12,067.38	5,387.22	179,071.26
44	12,534.99	5,776.49	185,829.76
45	13,008.08	6,194.33	192,643.51
46	13,485.05	6,642.88	199,485.68
47	13,964.00	7,124.49	206,325.19
48	14,442.76	7,641.67	213,126.28
49	14,918.84	8,197.16	219,847.96
50	15,389.36	8,793.92	226,443.40
51	15,851.04	9,435.14	232,859.30
52	16,300.15	10,124.32	239,035.13
53	16,732.46	10,865.23	244,902.36
54	17,143.17	11,662.02	250,383.51
55	17,526.85	12,519.18	255,391.18
56	17,877.38	13,441.64	259,826.92
57	18,187.88	14,434.83	263,579.97
58	18,450.60	15,504.70	266,525.87

cont'd

(continued from previous page)

Year	Earnings	Required Minimum Distribution	Balance
59	18,656.81	16,657.87	268,524.81
60	18,796.74	17,901.65	269,419.90
61	18,859.39	19,244.28	269,035.01
62	18,832.45	20,695.00	267,172.46
63	18,702.07	22,264.37	263,610.16
64	18,452.71	23,964.56	258,098.31
65	18,066.88	25,809.83	250,355.36
66	17,524.88	27,817.26	240,062.98
67	16,804.41	30,007.87	226,859.52
68	15,880.17	32,408.50	210,331.19
69	14,723.18	35,055.20	189,999.17
70	13,299.94	37,999.83	165,299.28
71	11,570.95	41,324.82	135,545.41
72	9,488.18	45,181.80	99,851.79
73	6,989.63	49,925.90	56,915.52
74	3,984.09	60,899.61	0.00
	709,908.09	731,908.09	

Question 5.43: *Jack Phillips has selected Craig as the designated beneficiary of his IRA in order to provide for Craig's future. He has selected Thomas Phillips, his son, as the Custodian for Craig until Craig's 18th birthday. In wording his protective election out of the five-year rule, Jack has focused on saving Craig federal income taxes. Has he saved Craig state income taxes as well?*

Answer: Probably. Most states have a state income tax. By mandating a distribution that is the greater of the required minimum distribution or $1,000 to be paid annually, Jack Phillips may have saved Craig state income taxes as well.

Question 5.44: *Why should Jack Phillips be concerned about Craig's potential state income taxes?*

Answer: Most states have a state income tax. State income tax rates generally are incremental in nature and may be significant if no effective tax planning is done.

Question 5.45: *Will state law allow an individual such as Craig, who may be claimed as a dependent on another's tax return, to claim an exemption deduction for himself on his own state income tax return?*

Answer: Maybe. It depends on the state income tax laws of the particular state. A number of states allow a single individual who may be claimed as a dependent the exemption deduction, but many states do not. For example, in Alabama, Arizona, Connecticut, Georgia, Louisiana, Massachusetts, and Mississippi a single individual is entitled to an exemption deduction that is well in excess of $1,000 per year, even if that individual may be claimed as a dependent. States that do not allow an exemption deduction to a single individual who may be claimed as a dependent include Colorado, Delaware, Georgia, Hawaii, Idaho, Illinois, and Kansas. New York State does not allow any taxpayer (adult or minor) to claim a personal exemption, but it does allow an exemption deduction for dependents claimed by the taxpayer.

Question 5.46: *Do states allow a standard deduction for a single individual who may be claimed as a dependent on another tax return?*

Answer: Maybe. Many states allow an individual who is single a significant standard deduction. Thus, a single individual may obtain a standard deduction that is well in excess of $1,000, even though that single person is also being claimed as another's dependent. This applies in such states as California, Georgia, Hawaii, Kansas, Louisiana, Mississippi, and North Carolina. However, a number of states limit the standard deduction in instances where a single individual can be claimed as a dependent of another. These states include Colorado, Idaho, Maine, Minnesota, Missouri, New Mexico, New York, and Oregon.

Question 5.47: *What type of state income tax structure do states use?*

Answer: State income tax rates vary from state to state. A few states like Florida, Nevada, South Dakota, and Texas have no state income tax. A number of states have a flat tax rate. Most states have incremental income tax rates.

Question 5.48: *Is Craig exposed to any significant state income tax liability based upon the annual distributions that Thomas Phillips, as Custodian received (including earnings)?*

Answer: Probably not. The typical state income tax law allows its taxpayers either a significant standard deduction or an exemption deduction, or possibly both deductions in determining the taxable income of its taxpayers. Basically, these deductions should eliminate between $1,500 and $3,000 of state gross income in many states.

Question 5.49: *Assume that Craig, now age 19, needs the balance from his grandfather Jack's IRA for a business that he plans to open within the next two years. If Craig is interested in minimizing his income tax liability after his 18th birthday, what course of action should he take?*

Answer: Craig should take the distributions from Jack's IRA during the next two years in amounts that will take advantage of the federal standard deduction, the 15% federal income tax rate, and the lowest state income tax rate.

Question 5.50: *How much of an income tax savings was accomplished by Jack Phillips' selection of Craig (through his Custodian Thomas) as the designated beneficiary of his IRA as opposed to selecting his son, Thomas, directly as the designated beneficiary?*

Answer: The income tax savings are significant. Let us assume that Thomas Phillips is in the 31% federal income tax bracket and that Thomas lives in State X where he is in the 6% state income tax bracket. Since the 6% state income tax is deductible on his federal income tax return, Thomas Phillips has an effective overall tax rate of approximately 35%.

Assume that Craig receives 12 annual distributions of $1,000 each from Jack's IRA. Approximately $9,600 of these distributions are tax free because of Craig's annual standard deduction. Craig receives approximately $5,500 of earnings on the distributions. He will pay approximately $1,200 in federal income tax on the taxable portion of his IRA distributions and the earnings on the distributions. No state income tax is applicable because of the state exemption deduction and/or the state standard deduction.

Had Thomas Phillips received the $12,000 directly he would have paid approximately $4,200 in federal and state income tax on the distributions. This is based upon the assumption that Thomas has an effective tax bracket of 35% (federal and state), which is applied to the 12 annual distributions of $1,000. In addition, Thomas Phillips would receive approximately $3,000 of earnings, and not the $5,500 of earnings that Craig received. The reason for the lower earnings is that Thomas Phillips will pay more taxes than Craig and, therefore, have less money working for him. The $3,000 of earnings is taxable to Thomas Phillips at 35% or $1,050. The total tax liability on the $12,000 of distributions and $3,000 of earnings at 35% is $5,250. Thus, Thomas Phillips will pay approximately $4,050 more in federal and state income tax on the first $12,000 of IRA distributions than will Craig. This is computed as follows:

Approximate taxes paid by Thomas Phillips on the $12,000 of IRA distributions	$4,200
Approximate taxes paid by Thomas Phillips on the earnings of $3,000	1,050
Total approximate taxes paid by Thomas Phillips	$5,250
Approximate taxes paid by Craig on the $12,000 of IRA distributions and on the earnings of $5,500	1,200
Additional taxes paid by Thomas Phillips	$4,050

Question 5.51: *Assume that Craig decides to take the balance of Jack's IRA of $31,659.76 plus earnings thereon (see answer to Question 5.39) in two equal installments of approximately $17,600. Assume that Craig's overall effective federal and state income tax rate is 18%. What is Craig's tax liability on these two distributions of $17,600?*

Answer: Craig's tax liability is $3,168 for each year or a total of $6,336 for both years. Each $17,600 IRA distribution is subject to an 18% effective tax rate.

Question 5.52: *Assume in Question 5.51 that Thomas Phillips was the designated beneficiary and received these two equal distributions of $17,600. Thomas has an overall tax rate of 35%. What is the tax liability of Thomas on these two distributions of $17,600.*

Answer: Thomas would have a tax liability of $6,160 for each year or a total of $12,320 for both years. The $17,600 distribution for each year is subject to a 35% effective tax rate.

Question 5.53: Based upon your answers to Question 5.40, 5.50, 5.51 and 5.52, how much of an income tax savings is there if Craig Phillips (through his Custodian) is selected as the designated beneficiary of the IRA instead of Thomas directly?

Answer: The income tax savings is $10,034.

If Thomas Phillips was directly selected as the designated beneficiary then Thomas would have a tax liability of $17,150. This is computed as follows:

Answer to Question 5.50	$ 5,250
Answer to Question 5.52	12,320
Tax liability of Thomas Phillips	$17,570

If Craig was selected as the designated beneficiary, then Craig and his parents would have a tax liability of $7,536. This is computed as follows:

Answer to Question 5.40	$1,200
Answer to Question 5.51	6,336
Tax liability of Craig and his parents	$7,536

If Craig is the designated beneficiary instead of Thomas, then the tax savings is $10,034. This is computed as follows:

Tax liability of Thomas Phillips	$17,570
Tax liability of Craig Phillips and his parents	7,536
Difference	$10,034

Question 5.54: *Could the tax savings be greater than $10,034?*

Answer: Yes. If the remaining balance of $31,659.76 in Jack's IRA was paid to Craig over a period that exceeded the two-year period described above, then the tax-deferred growth would result in a greater overall tax savings.

Benefits of Irrevocable Trusts:

The following questions and answers will guide you in determining how an irrevocable trust can be used as an effective tool in retirement distribution planning for the family unit.

Question 5.55: *When should an irrevocable trust be used as the beneficiary of an IRA?*

Answer: An irrevocable trust should be considered when the designated beneficiary is a minor.

If there are several minors involved and the intended beneficiaries of your IRAs are minors, then it may be best for ease of administration that a separate irrevocable trust be set up for each minor's benefit.

Although that may seem to create more paperwork, it makes it easier to control the benefits that flow to the particular designated beneficiary. The IRS rules permit the use of the irrevocable trust in determining the period over which payments can be made to the individual who benefits from the irrevocable trust.

Question 5.56: *Why bother with an irrevocable trust if a Custodian under the Uniform Gifts to Minors Act can be used as the beneficiary on behalf of the minor?*

Answer: Depending on state law, the Custodian can only receive the IRA proceeds until either age 18 or 21. If there are significant sums of money involved, then those ages may not be appropriate since the funds must be turned over to the beneficiary at that point in time.

Question 5.57: *If an irrevocable trust for the benefit of the grandchild is to receive the IRA distributions, over how long a period may the trust last?*

Answer: The irrevocable trust may last as long as the life expectancy of the grandchild based upon the IRS life expectancy rules.

Question 5.58: *Donald Johnson, age 66 in 1997, has a considerable amount of assets as well as $300,000 in several IRAs. He has two grandchildren, Robert, age two, and Keith, age six. Donald would like to make both grandchildren the designated beneficiaries of one of his IRAs that contains $200,000. Should he do so?*

Answer: No. Since both grandchildren are minors and may be minors at the time of Donald's death, then the probate courts will become involved if he names the grandchildren directly as the designated beneficiaries of his IRA.

Question 5.59: *Assuming that Donald's grandchildren were age 18 and 24, should he name both grandchildren as the designated beneficiaries of one IRA?*

Answer: No. If both grandchildren are the designated beneficiaries of one IRA, then the younger grandchild is deemed to be the older grandchild's age for purposes of the IRS life expectancy payout rules. This age difference of six years can make a big difference in terms of the ultimate payout. The younger beneficiary is placed at a disadvantage by being deemed the age of the older beneficiary.

Question 5.60: *Is there a better approach that Donald could use to provide benefits to adult grandchildren?*

Answer: Yes. It is best that two IRAs of $100,000 each be established. Each adult grandchild should be the designated beneficiary of a separate IRA. This will result in some additional paperwork but in the long run it will permit greater tax planning opportunities on behalf of the younger designated beneficiary.

Question 5.61: *If Donald established an irrevocable trust for the benefit of Robert and an irrevocable trust for the benefit of Keith and named each irrevocable trust as the beneficiary of a separate IRA that contained $100,000, can Donald change the terms of the irrevocable trust?*

Answer: No. The terms of an irrevocable trust cannot be changed.

Question 5.62: *Does that mean that he cannot change his beneficiary designation?*

Answer: No. An irrevocable trust is not an irrevocable beneficiary. Donald can always change the beneficiary or designated beneficiary of his IRA as long as he is alive and competent to do so.

Question 5.63: *Can you illustrate the distinction between an irrevocable beneficiary and an irrevocable trust in the context of an IRA beneficiary?*

Answer: Yes. Assume that Donald establishes IRA No. 1 in the amount of $100,000 and selects the irrevocable trust for the benefit of Robert as the beneficiary of the death benefits of IRA No. 1. Donald later realizes that his son, Mark, is not doing well and will need the IRA death benefits. Donald can change the designated beneficiary of IRA No. 1 to Mark instead of the irrevocable trust for the benefit of Robert. Donald can always change his beneficiary or designated beneficiary during his lifetime.

Question 5.64: *Is a trust a beneficiary or a designated beneficiary?*

Answer: A trust is technically a beneficiary and not a designated beneficiary.

Question 5.65: *If Robert is the beneficiary of an irrevocable trust created by his grandfather Donald, is Robert considered to be a designated beneficiary for purposes of the IRS distribution rules?*

Answer: According to the IRS, if certain requirements are met, Robert is deemed to be a designated beneficiary even though he takes his distributions through a trust. The rules that must be followed are:

a. The trust is a valid trust under state law, or would be but for the fact that there is no corpus.

b. The trust is irrevocable.

c. The beneficiary of the trust is identifiable.

d. A copy of the trust instrument is provided to the IRA institution. In the opinion of the author the trust should be specifically referred to in the beneficiary forms that are on file with the IRA institution.

Question 5.66: *Under the first test in Question 5.65, what do the words "but for the fact that there is no corpus" mean?*

Answer: The language means that there need not be any assets in the trust before the IRA owner's date of death.

Question 5.67: *Are there any other reasons why Donald should consider selecting an irrevocable trust for the benefit of a grandchild as the beneficiary of his IRA?*

Answer: Yes. If the ultimate beneficiary of the irrevocable trust cannot handle funds, then the trustee of the irrevocable trust will protect the grandchild from making poor investment decisions and from dissipating the IRA assets over a short period of time. In addition, the trustee will protect the grandchild from the influence of third parties. The assets of the IRA will also be protected from the creditors of the grandchild. If the grandchild was the direct beneficiary of the IRA, then the IRA would be more vulnerable to creditors of the grandchild. Further, the trustee may consider the income tax liability of the grandchild in determining whether to accelerate distributions to the grandchild.

An irrevocable trust for a child may be established for the same reasons as described above.

Question 5.68: *Who should be the trustee of the irrevocable trust for the benefit of a grand-child?*

Answer: The trustee can be an institutional trustee or it can be a member of the family. If the irrevocable trust for the benefit of a grandchild is established by a grandfather, then he can name a series of trustees such as the grandmother as the first trustee, then a parent or parents of the grandchild, then an aunt or uncle or accountant or attorney as successor trustee.

Question 5.69: *How should the trustee be compensated?*

Answer: Since the trustee after the IRA owner's death controls the IRA investments and will have to maintain trust accounting records and file fiduciary income tax returns, then he should be compensated based upon the statutory fees under state law or fees as stated in the trust document. These fee arrangements should be spelled out in the trust document. Often, the trust document will provide that no trustee commissions shall be paid to the grandparents, the parents of the child or any other relatives who serve as trustee. The trust should provide that if a non-relative serves as trustee that such trustee shall receive the greater of the statutory fees under state law or the fees as stated in the trust document.

Question 5.70: *What other provisions should be provided in the trust document?*

Answer: Since the trustee of the irrevocable trust controls the IRA investments, he or she should be guided in terms of the characteristics of the investments that should be made. This may include the percentage of IRA assets that should be invested in fixed income instruments and equity investments and whether or not an investment advisor should be used for investing in equities. This is important, since the trustee could be vulnerable to a lawsuit by the beneficiary of the trust if poor investment decisions are made.

Question 5.71: *May the trust provide that the minor be made a trustee when he or she gets older?*

Answer: Yes. The trust document should provide that at a certain age the ultimate beneficiary shall become the trustee. For example, if the irrevocable trust is for the benefit of a minor and the IRA life expectancy for the minor is 70.7 years, then the trust should provide that at some age the beneficiary of the trust should become the trustee. The trust could state, for example, that at age 35, the beneficiary of the trust shall become the trustee.

Question 5.72: *May the trust provide for acceleration rights of distribution from the IRA?*

Answer: Yes. The trust may provide that the trustee can accelerate additional distributions from the IRA based upon a certain standard or for any reason. In addition, the trust must receive the required minimum distributions from the IRA each year.

Question 5.73: *Must the trustee pay out the distributions that it receives each year from the IRA to the beneficiary of the trust?*

Answer: It depends on the terms of the trust. If the trust instrument states that it must pay out all the distributions it receives annually to the beneficiary, then the trustee must follow the provisions of the trust document.

Question 5.74: *If the beneficiary of the trust is a minor, what provision should be made in the trust agreement in order to avoid the jurisdiction of the probate court?*

Answer: The trust instrument may state that if the beneficiary of the trust is a minor that the distribution may be withheld until the minor's 18th birthday or 21st birthday or that it may be paid to a Custodian under the Uniform Gifts to Minors Act or Uniform Transfers to Minors Act for the benefit of the minor during his minority.

Question 5.75: *Is there an income tax advantage if the trust receives substantial distributions from the IRA, and doesn't pay it out annually to the beneficiary?*

Answer: No. The Clinton income tax rates for trusts and estates are exceptionally high and run into the 39.6% bracket very quickly. If the beneficiary is over the age of 14, then a substantial amount of monies received by the beneficiary from the trustee may be taxed at 15% instead of 39.6%. If the trustee has discretion, then the trustee may timely pay out the income to the beneficiary of the trust in order to avoid the higher income tax that the trust would otherwise pay.

Question 5.76: *Is there a way to make sure that the income is taxed to the beneficiary of the trust in order to avoid the income tax problem described in Question 5.75?*

Answer: Yes. The trust may provide that all distributions it receives each year from the IRA must be paid out to the beneficiary each year.

Question 5.77: *Is there an estate tax savings to the estate of the deceased IRA owner if the IRA proceeds are payable to an irrevocable trust for the benefit of a child instead of directly to the child?*

Answer: No. The IRA is included in the gross estate of the deceased IRA owner. It makes no difference if the irrevocable trust is the beneficiary of the IRA or if the IRA is payable directly to the child.

Question 5.78: *Is there an estate tax liquidity problem that may be solved if the irrevocable trust receives the distributions before paying it to the child?*

Answer: Yes. Many taxpayers have estates that lack liquidity. If the IRA is subject to a significant estate tax liability, then the trustee of the irrevocable trust should be required to remit its share of the estate tax liability to the executor of the estate or directly to the IRS and state tax department if the beneficiary of the IRA refuses to contribute his or her share of estate taxes from other assets that he or she owns.

Question 5.79: *If the estate lacks liquidity, can the IRA be paid directly to the estate instead of having the IRA paid to the irrevocable trust and then having the trustee of the trust remit its share of estate taxes back to the estate?*

Answer: Yes. The IRA can be paid to the estate of the deceased IRA owner if the estate is selected as the beneficiary of the IRA. This approach should be used only if you suspect that the child will not pay his share of the estate taxes from other assets that he owns.

Question 5.80: *If the estate lacks liquidity is there an alternative approach to either selecting the trust or the estate as the beneficiary of the IRA?*

Answer: Yes. Multiple IRAs can be created. One IRA can name the estate as the beneficiary and the other IRA can name the child or an irrevocable trust for the child as the beneficiary.

Question 5.81: *If you have confidence in your child, can you name the child as the direct beneficiary of your IRA even if your estate lacks liquidity?*

Answer: Yes. However, the executor may have a problem if the child for whatever reason refuses to pay his or her share of the estate taxes that are attributable to the IRA.

Question 5.82: *If you have several children each of whom is a designated beneficiary of a separate IRA and your estate is not liquid, what approach should be used?*

Answer: If you think the children may refuse to use assets of their own to pay the estate taxes, you may have no choice but to establish a separate irrevocable trust for the benefit of each child so that the trustee of each trust may pay such child's share of the estate tax liability.

CHAPTER 6

Nonspouse Designated Beneficiary Who Is No More Than 10 Years Younger

We previously discussed the distribution rules that apply if you select a nonspouse designated beneficiary who is more than 10 years younger than yourself. If you select a nonspouse designated beneficiary who is no more than 10 years younger than you are or is older than you are, some of the rules change. If you die before your required beginning date, the nonspouse designated beneficiary rules discussed in earlier chapters are the same. However, the rules for calculating your required minimum distributions from your IRA are different when you attain your required beginning date. These rules are discussed in this chapter.

Where the nonspouse designated beneficiary is no more than 10 years younger than you are or older than you are, then the amount of your required minimum distributions each year depends on whether the term-certain method or a special hybrid method is used. The method used by you as the account owner will also affect the distribution rules for your designated beneficiary after your death.

These rules apply to IRAs, qualified plans, and 403(b) annuity contracts.

Taking into Account Designated Beneficiary's Life Expectancy:

The following questions and answers discuss how the choice of a nonspouse designated beneficiary affects the life expectancy period the account owner may use in determining his required minimum distributions.

Question 6.1: *Paul Wilson wants to select his brother Bernard as the designated beneficiary of his IRA. May Paul take advantage of the life expectancy of Bernard in determining his required minimum distributions?*

Answer: Yes. Paul may consider Bernard's life expectancy in determining his required minimum distributions provided that Bernard is selected as the designated beneficiary by Paul's required beginning date. Paul's required beginning date is April 1 of the calendar year following the calendar year in which he attains age $70^{1}/_{2}$.

Question 6.2: *In order to determine the joint life expectancy of Paul and Bernard, as of what year is the joint life expectancy determined?*

Answer: The calendar year in which the IRA owner attains age $70^{1}/_{2}$ is the year that the joint life expectancy is determined. We need to review how old Paul and Bernard are as of their birthdays in the year Paul attains age 70½. Assume that Paul's 70th birthday is May 5, 1997; he is age 70½ on November 5, 1997. Thus, for Paul, we use age 70. After that we determine Bernard's age on his birthday in the calendar year 1997. Assume that on his birthday in 1997 Bernard is age 62. Therefore, the joint life expectancy of Paul and Bernard under the IRS table is based upon combined ages of 70 and 62.

Question 6.3: *Based on their ages in 1997, what is the combined life expectancy of Paul and Bernard in order to determine Paul's required minimum distributions for his first distribution calendar year?*

Answer: Paul's first distribution calendar year is 1997, the first year for which he is required to receive a required minimum distribution under the IRS rules. The combined life expectancy of Paul and Bernard as of Paul's first distribution calendar year, based upon age 70 and 62, is 24.9 years. If Paul timely selects his brother, Bernard, as the designated beneficiary of his IRA by no later than his required beginning date, which is April 1, 1998, then he may use his brother's life expectancy in determining his required minimum distributions from his IRA. The joint life expectancy of Paul and Bernard is shown in Table II of IRS Publication 590, which is included in the Appendix of this book. The same IRS table is referred to as Table VI in Section 1.72–9 of the Income Tax Regulations.

Question 6.4: *Assume that Paul initially selected his estate as the beneficiary of his IRA as of his required beginning date. He then made Bernard the designated beneficiary of his IRA after his required beginning date. Must Paul use the single life expectancy table in determining his required minimum distributions from his IRA?*

Answer: Yes. Since Paul had selected his estate as the beneficiary of his IRA as of his required beginning date, then he must use the single life expectancy table in calculating the required minimum distributions from his IRA. The subsequent selection of his brother, Bernard, as the designated beneficiary of his IRA after his required beginning date comes too late in the game.

Question 6.5: *May Paul change the beneficiary to designated beneficiary of his IRA after his required beginning date?*

Answer: Yes. One can always change a beneficiary or designated beneficiary of an IRA at any time. However, for purposes of figuring required minimum distributions, the IRS life expectancy rules that are described in this book depend on who is the designated beneficiary of the IRA owner as of the IRA owner's required beginning date.

Question 6.6: *Assume that as of December 31, 1997, Paul had selected his estate as the beneficiary of his IRA. Paul selects his brother, Bernard as the designated beneficiary of his*

IRA by his required beginning date of April 1, 1998. May Paul take advantage of the IRS joint life expectancy tables in calculating his required minimum distribution for the calendar year 1997?

Answer: Yes. The IRS rules state that an IRA owner may select his designated beneficiary by no later than his required beginning date, which here is April 1, 1998. Paul can anticipate the fact that he will select Bernard as his designated beneficiary by no later than his required beginning date of April 1, 1998. Therefore, Paul may calculate his required minimum distribution for the calendar year 1997 based upon an IRS joint life expectancy period of 24.9 years. If Bernard should die before April 1, 1998, then Paul may select another designated beneficiary by that date or leave his estate as his beneficiary. If Paul should leave his estate as his beneficiary as of his required beginning date, then he must receive his required minimum distribution for the calendar year 1997 by no later than April 1, 1998, based upon a single life expectancy of 16 years, the single life expectancy of a 70 year old under IRS Table I from Publication 590, shown in the Appendix of this book.

Question 6.7:   *Assume that Paul's IRA account balance as of December 31, 1996 is $96,000. During the calendar year 1997 Paul selected his estate as his beneficiary, but he anticipates selecting his brother, Bernard, as his designated beneficiary by no later than April 1, 1998, Paul's required beginning date. How much must Paul receive from his IRA for the calendar year 1997 to avoid an IRS penalty, based upon his anticipated selection of his brother Bernard as his designated beneficiary?*

Answer: $3,855.42. Paul's first distribution calendar year is 1997. In order to determine his required minimum distribution for the first distribution calendar year 1997, Paul must use the value of his IRA account balance as of the end of the prior year which is divided by the appropriate life expectancy that is applicable to the first distribution calendar year 1997. The account balance as of December 31, 1996 of $96,000 is divided by 24.9 years, which is based upon Paul selecting Bernard as his designated beneficiary by April 1, 1998, Paul's required beginning date. The result is $3,855.42.

Question 6.8:   *Assume that Paul timely selects his brother, Bernard, as the designated beneficiary of his IRA. Also assume that the IRA plan document is liberal and permits Paul to elect the term-certain method by no later than his required beginning date. If Paul wishes to elect a term-certain method what should he do?*

Answer: Paul should timely elect in writing to use the term-certain method. He should send off a letter, certified return receipt requested to his IRA institution so that it is received by the IRA institution by no later than his required beginning date. Paul should elect the maximum term-certain period of 24.9 years, since he may always accelerate distributions from time to time. However, if he wishes he may elect a term-certain period of 24 years for convenience purposes. The maximum term-certain period of 24.9 years is the joint life expectancy of Paul and Bernard as of the year Paul attains age $70^1/_2$; see Question 6.3.

Question 6.9: *Assume that Paul timely selected Bernard as the designated beneficiary of his IRA. Also assume that Paul timely elects the term-certain method without specifying the term-certain period. Would the term-certain period be deemed to be 24.9 years?*

Answer: Probably. The IRS has not issued any guidelines on the mechanics of making the election. As a result the IRS letter rulings have been liberal in nature and reasonable in their interpretation of the distribution rules where possible. Therefore the 24.9 year term-certain period would probably be deemed to have been automatically elected.

Question 6.10: *Assume that Paul timely selected Bernard as the designated beneficiary of his IRA. Also assume that Paul timely elected a 20-year term-certain period by his required beginning date. Could he later change his mind after his required beginning date and switch to 24.9 years as the term-certain period?*

Answer: In the absence of an IRS letter ruling that permits this change it should not be done. The IRS has stated the following in the case of annuity distributions from a defined benefit plan:

"Once payments have commenced over a period certain, the period certain may not be lengthened even if the period certain is shorter than the maximum permitted."

Question 6.11: *Based upon the answer to Question 6.10, what should Paul do if he wishes to maximize the term-certain period?*

Answer: Paul should timely elect the maximum term-certain period by his required beginning date in order to play it safe. He can round down the maximum period if he wishes. If he merely elects the term-certain method without specifying a term-certain period, then the IRS will probably have no alternative but to permit him to automatically use the maximum term-certain period. Paul should not elect a term-certain period of 20 years and then hope to expand it at a later date. There is currently no authority to allow a subsequent expansion of the distribution period from 20 years to 24.9 years after the required beginning date.

Question 6.12: *Assume that Paul selected his brother Bernard as the designated beneficiary of his IRA by his required beginning date. If Paul timely elected to receive his required minimum distributions over a term-certain period of 24.9 years, what life expectancy period would he use during his first seven distribution calendar years in determining his required minimum distributions?*

Answer: The following schedule indicates the life expectancy period that Paul would use under the term-certain method. As you can see, the term-certain period decreases by one with each distribution calendar year.

Paul's Age	Distribution Year	Distribution Calendar Year	Term-Certain Method Life Expectancy Period
70	1	1997	24.9
71	2	1998	23.9
72	3	1999	22.9
73	4	2000	21.9
74	5	2001	20.9
75	6	2002	19.9
76	7	2003	18.9

Question 6.13: *Assume that Paul timely selected his brother Bernard as the designated beneficiary of his IRA by no later than his required beginning date of April 1, 1998. Also assume that Paul timely elected with the IRA institution to receive his required minimum distributions from the IRA over a term-certain period of 24.9 years. May Paul accelerate distributions from his IRA from time to time?*

Answer: Yes. Nothing prevents Paul from accelerating his distributions from his IRA from time to time. The law only provides that Paul must receive annual required minimum distributions from his IRA in order to avoid the 50% penalty that is applicable to a shortfall in a required minimum distribution.

Question 6.14: *Assume that Bernard dies on March 1, 1998. Paul then selects his estate as the beneficiary of his IRA. He withdrew $3,855.42 from his IRA during his first distribution calendar year 1997. What should Paul do in order to avoid any penalty with respect to his required minimum distribution for his first distribution calendar year 1997?*

Answer: Paul has until April 1, 1998 to take his required minimum distribution for his first distribution calendar year 1997. Paul's required distribution for the calendar year 1997 would be $6,000, equal to his $96,000 account balance as of December 31, 1996, divided by 16 years. This 16-year period is based upon the single life expectancy of Paul. Since Paul received $3,855.42 during his first distribution calendar year 1997, he must receive an additional $2,144.58 by no later than April 1, 1998 in order to avoid any 50% penalty. The difference between $6,000 and $3,855.42 is $2,144.58, which is the balance that is necessary in order to satisfy the required minimum distribution for the first distribution calendar year 1997. This will avoid any IRS penalty.

Distributions to a Nonspouse Designated Beneficiary Under Term-Certain Method Following Required Beginning Date:

The following questions and answers consider the manner in which a nonspouse designated beneficiary must receive required minimum distributions following the account owner's death, assuming the owner had timely elected the term-certain method.

Question 6.15: *Assume that Paul having timely selected Bernard as his designated beneficiary elected a term-certain period of 24.9 years over which to receive his required minimum distributions from his IRA. Also assume that Paul died in 2003 at age 76. The year 2003 is Paul's seventh distribution calendar year. He received his required minimum distribution for his seventh distribution calendar year 2003 before the date of his death. Assume that Bernard survived Paul and is still the designated beneficiary of Paul's IRA. When must Bernard commence his required minimum distributions from Paul's IRA?*

Answer: Bernard must commence his required minimum distributions from Paul's IRA starting in the calendar year following Paul's year of death. This is necessary in order for Bernard to satisfy the required minimum distribution rules that are now applicable to Bernard upon Paul's death.

Question 6.16: *Based upon the facts in Question 6.15, over how many years may Bernard receive required minimum distributions from Paul's IRA?*

Answer: Bernard may receive required minimum distributions from Paul's IRA over a 17.9 year term-certain period. This is based upon the fact that Paul elected a 24.9 year term-certain period over which to receive required minimum distributions from his IRA and seven years have elapsed in the 24.9 year term-certain period. The balance of the term-certain period that Bernard may use is 17.9 years.

Question 6.17: *Assume the facts in Question 6.15. Also assume that Paul's IRA account balance as of December 31, 2003 is $85,000. How much must Bernard receive from Paul's IRA during the calendar year 2004 in order to satisfy the IRS required minimum distribution rules?*

Answer: $4,748.60. Bernard calculates his required minimum distribution from Paul's IRA by dividing Paul's IRA account balance as of December 31, 2003 of $85,000 by the 17.9 years that remains in the initial term-certain period of 24.9 years. The result is $4,748.60.

Question 6.18: *Under the facts in Question 6.15, Bernard may receive required minimum distributions over a term-certain period of 17.9 years following Paul's death, but may Bernard accelerate distributions from Paul's IRA from time to time?*

Answer: Yes. Nothing prevents Bernard from accelerating distributions from Paul's IRA from time to time. The law only requires that Bernard must receive required minimum distributions annually from Paul's IRA in order to avoid the 50% penalty that is applicable to a shortfall in a required minimum distribution.

Question 6.19: *Assume that Bernard died after receiving required minimum distributions from Paul's IRA over a five-year period. Who would receive required minimum distributions from Paul's IRA after the death of Bernard?*

Answer: Bernard's estate. In the absence of any subsequent direction by Bernard, the required minimum distributions of Paul's IRA would be paid to Bernard's estate. This is a matter of state law and not IRS rules. The required minimum distributions are governed by IRS rules. However property rights are governed by state law.

Question 6.20: *Over what period of time would Bernard's estate receive required minimum distributions from Paul's IRA?*

Answer: Bernard's estate would receive required minimum distributions from Paul's IRA over a 12.9-year period. This is based upon the fact that there is only 12.9 years left in the initial 24.9-year term-certain period. This is computed as follows:

Initial term-certain period elected by Paul	24.9 years
Less: Years used by Paul	(7.0) years
Years used by Bernard	(5.0) years
Balance of term-certain period	12.9 years

Question 6.21: *May Bernard's estate accelerate distributions from Paul's IRA from time to time?*

Answer: Yes. Nothing prevents Bernard's estate from accelerating distributions from Paul's IRA from time to time.

Question 6.22: *Assume that Bernard's executor does not wish to keep Bernard's estate open for 12.9 years in order to receive required minimum distributions from Paul's IRA. What options are available to Bernard's executor?*

Answer: Bernard's executor may either accelerate the distributions from Paul's IRA to Bernard's estate or assign the rights to the future payments from Paul's IRA to the beneficiaries of Bernard's estate.

Question 6.23: *Which option is better?*

Answer: It is generally better to assign the future payments to the beneficiaries of Bernard's estate if the amounts are significant.

Question 6.24: *Before assigning the future payments from Paul's IRA to the beneficiaries of Bernard's estate, what action should Bernard's executor take?*

Answer: He should discuss the assignment approach with the IRA institution and beneficiaries to make certain that they understand it. In addition, the IRA institution should agree in writing that it will honor the assignment of the IRA payments to the heirs of Bernard's estate.

Question 6.25: *Assume that the heirs of Bernard's estate are assigned the remaining future installment payments from Paul's IRA. May the beneficiaries accelerate the payments from Paul's IRA from time to time?*

Answer: Yes. However, if some of the beneficiaries of Bernard's estate wish to accelerate payments from Paul's IRA from time to time while others do not, then a problem may arise in the accounting for the distributions from Paul's IRA. In that case it is best that a number of IRAs then be established and maintained in Paul's name. Each beneficiary of Bernard's estate will then control an IRA that has been allocated to him or her.

Question 6.26: *Is there any other reason for establishing a separate IRA that is maintained in Paul's name for each beneficiary of Bernard's estate?*

Answer: Yes. It is possible that each beneficiary may have a different investment philosophy in investing Paul's IRA funds. By separating IRAs a potential conflict in investment philosophy is avoided.

Question 6.27: *Can you think of any other reason for splitting up IRAs so that each beneficiary controls his or her allocated share of Paul's IRA?*

Answer: The IRA institution may only be able to use the social security number of one beneficiary for purposes of reporting annual distributions on Form 1099-R. By having separate IRAs in Paul's name, each beneficiary will receive a separate Form 1099-R.

Question 6.28: *Assume that Bernard survives Paul. Bernard is not sophisticated in financial matters and has Paul's IRA retitled into his own name. Will there be a tax problem as a result of the change in the name of Paul's IRA account into Bernard's name?*

Answer: Yes. The IRA institution will issue a Form 1099-R to Bernard and he will have instant taxable income on Paul's entire IRA account balance. It is as if the entire balance had been distributed to Bernard. Bernard is not permitted to roll over Paul's IRA.

Question 6.29: *What should Bernard do in order to prevent the tax problem discussed in Question 6.28?*

Answer: Paul's IRA must be maintained in Paul's name. Paul's IRA should indicate that Paul is deceased and indicate the date of Paul's death. In addition, Bernard's social security number should be used on Paul's IRA account for tax purposes.

Question 6.30: *Assume that Paul elected a term-certain period of 24.9 years over which to receive his IRA distributions. Also assume that Paul died in 2003 at age 76. The year 2003 is Paul's seventh distribution calendar year. However, Paul died before he received his required minimum distribution for his seventh distribution calendar year. Bernard survived Paul and is still the designated beneficiary of Paul's IRA. What action should Bernard take after Paul's death?*

Answer: As soon as Bernard ascertains that Paul did not receive his required minimum distribution for year 2003, Bernard should withdraw that amount from Paul's IRA within a reasonable period of time. Bernard by law is entitled to the distribution since he is Paul's designated beneficiary. The distribution for the year 2003 would be based on a term-certain period of 18.9 years, since six years had elapsed in the 24.9-year term-certain period elected by Paul. The required minimum distribution for 2003 that Bernard should withdraw is the IRA account balance as of December 31, 2002, divided by 18.9.

This withdrawal by Bernard for the year of Paul's death is necessary in order to avoid any possible penalty by the IRS. The law permits Paul to receive the required minimum distribution for the year 2003 by December 31, 2003. If Paul dies before that date, the IRS will not assert any penalty for the failure of Paul to receive his required minimum distribution for the calendar year 2003. However, Bernard should receive Paul's required minimum distribution for the calendar year 2003 within a reasonable period of time in order to avoid any possible penalty.

In addition, Bernard must commence his required minimum distributions from Paul's IRA starting in the calendar year 2004 and for each calendar year thereafter for the remaining 17.9 year term-certain period. Bernard may accelerate distributions from Paul's IRA from time to time.

Question 6.31: *Assume that Paul had timely elected the term-certain method in determining his required minimum distributions from his IRA. Also assume that Paul dropped Bernard as the designated beneficiary of his IRA in the calendar year 2000 and selected his own estate as the beneficiary of his IRA in the calendar year 2000. What life expectancy would Paul use in determining his required minimum distributions from his IRA for the first seven distribution calendar years under the term-certain method?*

Answer: The following schedule indicates the period of time that Paul may use in determining his required minimum distributions from his IRA under the term-certain method as a result of dropping Bernard as his designated beneficiary in the calendar year 2000. Paul selected his estate as the beneficiary of his IRA in the calendar year 2000.

Paul's Age	Distribution Year	Calendar Year	Term-Certain Method
70	1	1997	24.9
71	2	1998	23.9
72	3	1999	22.9
73	4	2000	21.9
74	5	2001	12.0
75	6	2002	11.0
76	7	2003	10.0

Question 6.32: *Why must Paul use a shorter life expectancy under the term-certain method for the calendar year 2001 and thereafter?*

Answer: The IRS has special rules that are triggered if the IRA owner changes a designated beneficiary while the designated beneficiary is still alive. Paul may no longer use Bernard's life expectancy as of the calendar year following the calendar year in which Bernard was dropped as a designated beneficiary. In the calendar year 2000, Paul selected his estate as the beneficiary of his IRA in the calendar year 2000. Paul had timely elected the term-certain method in determining his required minimum distributions from his IRA. He must continue to use the term-certain method even though he may not take advantage of Bernard's life expectancy as of the calendar year 2001 and thereafter. Paul must revert to a single life expectancy as of the calendar year 2001 based upon a term-certain period. Paul must determine his single life expectancy in the calendar year that he attained age $70^1/_2$. Since Paul was age 70 in 1997, the year he attained age $70^1/_2$, his single life expectancy under Table V of section 1.72–9 of the Income Tax Regulations is 16 years as of the calendar year 1997. This life expectancy table is shown in the Appendix of this book as Table I of IRS Publication 590. As of the calendar year 2001 the remaining term-certain period that is available to Paul is 12 years. It is reduced by one for each year thereafter.

Question 6.33: *Assume that Paul died in the calendar year 2003 after receiving his required minimum distribution from his IRA for the calendar year 2003. Further assume that the term-certain method was applicable and that Bernard was dropped as Paul's designated beneficiary in the calendar year 2000. Paul's estate was selected as the beneficiary of Paul's IRA during the calendar year 2000. Over what period of time may Paul's estate receive required minimum distributions from Paul's IRA account?*

Answer: Since Paul timely elected the term-certain method, his estate may continue to receive distributions from his IRA over the balance of the term-certain period. In the calendar year 2003 Paul's term-certain period is 10 years (Question 6.31). Therefore, Paul's estate may receive required minimum distributions from Paul's IRA over the remaining nine-year period commencing in the calendar year 2004.

Question 6.34: *Assume that Paul timely selected Bernard as the designated beneficiary of his IRA. In the calendar year 2000 Paul dropped Bernard as his designated beneficiary and immediately substituted his other brother, Michael, as his designated beneficiary. Michael is two years younger than Bernard. May Paul take advantage of Michael's life expectancy in determining his required minimum distributions from his IRA?*

Answer: No. A special rule applies if a younger designated beneficiary replaces an older designated beneficiary after an IRA owner's required beginning date. The life expectancy of the older designated beneficiary is used even though the older designated beneficiary is no longer the designated beneficiary of the IRA owner. Thus, Michael is deemed to be the same age of Bernard and Michael's younger age is ignored.

Hybrid Method of Figuring Required Minimum Distributions if Term-Certain Method Not Elected:

If the IRA account owner does not elect the term-certain method of calculating required minimum distributions by the required beginning date, then a more complicated "hybrid" method must be used. This hybrid method is explained in the following questions and answers.

Question 6.35: *Assume that Paul selected Bernard as the designated beneficiary of his IRA as of his required beginning date but failed to elect the term-certain method of distribution. What is the effect of Paul's failure to elect the term-certain method of distribution?*

Answer: The distribution rules become much more complex. The law states that the IRA owner may recalculate his or her life expectancy each year but the nonspouse designated beneficiary's life expectancy may not be recalculated.

Question 6.36: *What does recalculation of life expectancy mean?*

Answer: Recalculation of life expectancy means that when the owner looks up life expectancy in the IRS tables, the owner's age on his or her birthday in each year is used. For example, in his first distribution calendar year of 1997, Paul is age 70 (see Question 6.2). If the recalculation method applies, then for the second distribution calendar year of 1998, Paul's age is 71 when applying the IRS life expectancy tables. For each subsequent year, Paul's age continues to increase by one year and the life expectancy for that age is used.

Question 6.37: *How do we know if the IRA owner Paul must recalculate his life expectancy each year?*

Answer: The IRA plan document must be consulted in order to determine whether or not the term-certain method could have been timely elected by Paul. The IRA plan document may specify whether or not the life expectancy of Paul must be recalculated in the event that Paul fails to make a timely election of a distribution method. If the IRA plan document is silent concerning distribution methods, then under the IRS rules, Paul must automatically default into the recalculation method as far as his own life expectancy is concerned. The recalculation method is not applicable to a nonspouse designated beneficiary.

Question 6.38: *Assume that Paul defaults into the recalculation method in calculating his required minimum distributions. Also assume that Bernard has been timely selected as the designated beneficiary of Paul's IRA. What is the method that is used in determining Paul's required minimum distributions each year?*

Answer: It is neither the term-certain method nor the recalculation method. It is a hybrid method for determining Paul's required minimum distributions from his IRA. The hybrid method recalculates Paul's life expectancy each year but uses a term-certain method with respect to Bernard's life expectancy.

Question 6.39: *Would you please indicate the applicable life expectancy that would be used by Paul in determining his required minimum distributions from his IRA for the first seven calendar years if he defaulted into the hybrid method?*

Answer: The following schedule reflects the life expectancy that Paul would use under the hybrid method.

Paul's Age	Distribution Year	Calendar Year	Hybrid Method
70	1	1997	24.9
71	2	1998	23.4
72	3	1999	22.5
73	4	2000	21.6
74	5	2001	20.8
75	6	2002	19.3
76	7	2003	18.5

Question 6.40: *How did you arrive at the life expectancy that was determined under the hybrid method as described in your answer to Question 6.39?*

Answer: The special IRS hybrid method rules apply if an individual has a nonspouse designated beneficiary who is no more than 10 years younger than the IRA owner, unless the owner has timely elected the term-certain method. Bernard is a nonspouse designated beneficiary of Paul's IRA and is eight years younger than Paul. Since Paul failed to timely elect the term-certain method with the IRA institution and defaulted into the hybrid method, the IRS special rules must be followed.

The computation of joint life expectancy under the hybrid method is complicated, and it may be advisable to obtain the assistance of a tax professional.

Question 6.41: *Assume that Paul timely selected his brother Bernard as the designated beneficiary of his IRA. Can you please compare the applicable life expectancy that would be used by Paul in determining his required minimum distributions from his IRA for the first seven distribution calendar years under the hybrid method and under the term-certain method?*

Answer: The following schedule reflects the comparison of the hybrid method and the term-certain method. Although the applicable life expectancy under the two methods is practically the same, the hybrid computation is much more complicated, as discussed in the answer to Question 6.40.

Paul's Age	Distribution Year	Calendar Year	Hybrid Method	Term-Certain Method
70	1	1997	24.9	24.9
71	2	1998	23.4	23.9
72	3	1999	22.5	22.9
73	4	2000	21.6	21.9
74	5	2001	20.8	20.9
75	6	2002	19.3	19.9
76	7	2003	18.5	18.9

Question 6.42: *Assume that Paul timely selected Bernard as the designated beneficiary of his IRA. For the years 1997 through 2003, Paul receives required minimum distributions using the hybrid method. During the calendar year 2003, Paul dies after receiving his required minimum distribution for the calendar year 2003. Assume that Bernard survives Paul. Over what period of time may Bernard receive his required minimum distributions under the hybrid method after the death of Paul?*

Answer: The IRS has special rules that apply in order to determine the period of time that Bernard may receive his required minimum distributions under the hybrid method. Bernard must initially determine his single life expectancy under the IRS life expectancy tables in the calendar year that Paul attained age 70$\frac{1}{2}$. In the year that Paul attained age 70$\frac{1}{2}$ Bernard was age 62. The single life expectancy of an individual age 62 under Table V of 1.72–9 of the Income Tax Regulations is 22.5 years. This table is shown in the Appendix of this book as Table I from IRS Publication 590. That 22.5-year period is used in calculating the life expectancy that can be used by Bernard after the year of death of Paul. Since Paul lived for seven distribution calendar years, seven years is subtracted from the 22.5-year period in order to determine the remaining period that can be used by Bernard in determining his required minimum distributions from Paul's IRA. Thus, Bernard may receive his required minimum distributions from Paul's IRA over 15.5 years starting in the calendar year 2004.

Question 6.43: *Assume that Paul died in the calendar year 2003 and that Bernard, his designated IRA beneficiary, survives him. Paul received his required minimum distribution for 2003 before he died. Would you please compare the remaining period that Bernard could use in determining his required minimum distributions under the hybrid method versus the term-certain method over a 12-year period commencing in 2004?*

Answer: The following schedule indicates the difference in the remaining period that can be used by Bernard under the hybrid method versus the term-certain method. The hybrid method applies unless Paul elected the term-certain method by his required beginning date of April 1, 1998. Bernard must commence his required minimum distributions from Paul's IRA in 2004, the calendar year following the year of Paul's death.

Bernard's Age	Distribution Year	Calendar Year	Hybrid Method	Term-Certain Method
69	1	2004	15.5	17.9
70	2	2005	14.5	16.9
71	3	2006	13.5	15.9
72	4	2007	12.5	14.9
73	5	2008	11.5	13.9
74	6	2009	10.5	12.9
75	7	2010	9.5	11.9
76	8	2011	8.5	10.9
77	9	2012	7.5	9.9
78	10	2013	6.5	8.9
79	11	2014	5.5	7.9
80	12	2015	4.5	6.9

Question 6.44: *Assume that Bernard died in the calendar year 2015 after receiving his required minimum distribution for the year 2015. Over what period of time may Bernard's estate receive required minimum distributions from Paul's IRA?*

Answer: That depends upon whether or not the hybrid method or term-certain method of distribution was used in determining Paul's required minimum distributions. Under the hybrid method Bernard's estate could receive required minimum distributions from

Paul's IRA over a 3.5-year period starting in 2016. If the term-certain was applicable, then Bernard's estate could receive required minimum distributions from Paul's IRA over a 5.9-year period starting in 2016. The difference between both methods is 2.4 years.

Question 6.45: *Assume that Paul had timely selected Bernard as the designated beneficiary of his IRA. Paul failed to timely elect the term-certain method and therefore defaulted into the hybrid method. Further assume that Bernard, his designated beneficiary, died in Paul's fourth distribution calendar year 2000. Would you please tell me over what period of time Paul may use in determining his required minimum distributions from his IRA under the hybrid method for the calendar years 1997 through 2003?*

Answer: The following schedule indicates the period of time that Paul may use in determining his required minimum distributions from his IRA under the hybrid method even though Bernard died in the calendar year 2000.

Paul's Age	Distribution Year	Calendar Year	Hybrid Method
70	1	1997	24.9
71	2	1998	23.4
72	3	1999	22.5
73	4	2000	21.6
74	5	2001	20.8
75	6	2002	19.3
76	7	2003	18.5

Question 6.46: *Your answer to Question 6.45 is the same as your answer to Question 6.39. Can you explain why your answer to each question is the same?*

Answer: Yes. According to the IRS, if Bernard is the designated beneficiary of Paul's IRA as of Paul's required beginning date, then Bernard's remaining life expectancy is fixed and can be used by Paul after Bernard dies.

Question 6.47: *May Paul change his beneficiary of his IRA to his estate after Bernard dies and still take advantage of Bernard's life expectancy in determining his required minimum distributions?*

Answer: Yes. The calculation that is made for Paul's required minimum distributions after Bernard's death is made as if Bernard was still alive. Once again, Bernard's remaining life expectancy is fixed and Bernard's death will not result in a change in the payout period.

Question 6.48: *Assume that Bernard did not die but that Paul eliminated Bernard as the designated beneficiary of his IRA in the calendar year 2000. Paul selects his estate as the beneficiary of his IRA in the calendar year 2000. Would your answer to Question 6.47 change?*

Answer: Yes. If Paul drops Bernard as his designated beneficiary while Bernard is alive in the calendar year 2000 and selects his own estate as the beneficiary of his IRA, then Paul loses the benefit of Bernard's life expectancy in the calendar year 2001 and for all calendar years thereafter.

Question 6.49: *Assume that Paul dropped Bernard as the designated beneficiary of his IRA in the calendar year 2000 and selected his estate as the beneficiary of his IRA in the calendar year 2000. Further assume that the hybrid method was applicable. Could you please indicate the life expectancy that would be used by Paul in determining his required minimum distributions from his IRA for the first seven distribution calendar years under the hybrid method?*

Answer: The following schedule indicates the period of time that Paul may use in determining his required minimum distributions from his IRA under the hybrid method as a result of dropping Bernard as his designated beneficiary in the calendar year 2000. Paul selected his estate as the beneficiary of his IRA in the calendar year 2000.

Paul's Age	Distribution Year	Calendar Year	Hybrid Method
70	1	1997	24.9
71	2	1998	23.4
72	3	1999	22.5
73	4	2000	21.6
74	5	2001	13.2
75	6	2002	12.5
76	7	2003	11.9

Question 6.50: *Based upon the facts in Question 6.49, why is there such a dramatic drop in the life expectancy table that Paul may use under the hybrid method for the calendar year 2001 and calendar years thereafter?*

Answer: Paul may not use Bernard's remaining life expectancy starting in the calendar year 2001 and calendar years thereafter. Since Paul is under the hybrid method he must use the recalculation method based upon his single life expectancy. The single life expectancy table from IRS Publication 590, shown in the Appendix of this book provides the single life expectancy that Paul must use for the calendar year 2001 and calendar years thereafter. The table from IRS Publication 590 is based upon Table V of Section 1.72–9 of the Income Tax Regulations. Each year his life expectancy is recalculated and used in determining his required minimum distributions from his IRA.

Question 6.51: *Assume the facts in Question 6.49 but then Paul dies in 2003. When must Paul's estate receive Paul's IRA account?*

Answer: Paul's life expectancy under the recalculation method is reduced to zero in the calendar year following his year of death. Since Paul died during the calendar year 2003, Paul's estate must receive his entire IRA account balance during the period between January 1, 2004 through December 30, 2004.

CHAPTER 7

The Estate as IRA or Qualified Plan Beneficiary

Most IRA owners and plan participants designate specific beneficiaries for their retirement plans and IRA accounts. Generally, it is preferable to timely select a designated beneficiary because the selection of a designated beneficiary will allow a longer life expectancy period for the payout of plan or IRA benefits. These life expectancy rules have been discussed in the previous chapters that relate to specific types of beneficiaries. However, in the event that the IRA owner or plan participant does not select anyone to benefit from his retirement benefits, then the estate becomes the beneficiary. This chapter will review the lifetime required minimum distribution rules for IRA owners and plan participants who select their estates as their beneficiaries, as well as the distribution rules for the estate following the death of the IRA owner or plan participant.

Question 7.1: *Why is it beneficial to timely select a designated beneficiary of my retirement plan assets?*

Answer: The timely selection of the designated beneficiary is important because the life expectancy of the designated beneficiary is considered in determining the calculation of the required minimum distributions that must be paid to you on and after your required beginning date which is April 1 of the year following the calendar year in which you attain age 70$^{1}/_{2}$. In addition, the life expectancy of a designated beneficiary is considered in determining the calculation of the required minimum distributions that must be paid to the designated beneficiary after your death.

Question 7.2: *Is an estate considered to be a designated beneficiary?*

Answer: No. An estate is considered a beneficiary but not a designated beneficiary. Only an individual may be a designated beneficiary.

Recalculation Method and Term-Certain Method:

The following questions and answers explain how to figure the amount of required minimum distributions under the recalculation and term-certain methods if an estate is the beneficiary, and how the choice of methods also affects distributions to your estate after your death.

Question 7.3: *Assume that Marshall Jones attains age 70¹/₂ in the calendar year 1997. He is single and has selected his estate as the beneficiary of his IRA. He fails to timely elect the term-certain method by his required beginning date of April 1, 1998. The IRA plan document states that the recalculation method is applicable if the IRA owner fails to timely elect not to use the recalculation method. Assume that Marshall lives until age 90. Can you please indicate what the life expectancy is for Marshall for each distribution calendar year under the recalculation method?*

Answer: If the recalculation method applies, the following schedule reflects the life expectancy period that Marshall would use to compute his required minimum distributions until age 90.

Recalculation Method

Marshall's Age	Distribution Year	Calendar Year	Life Expectancy
70	1	1997	16.0
71	2	1998	15.3
72	3	1999	14.6
73	4	2000	13.9
74	5	2001	13.2
75	6	2002	12.5
76	7	2003	11.9
77	8	2004	11.2
78	9	2005	10.6
79	10	2006	10.0
80	11	2007	9.5
81	12	2008	8.9
82	13	2009	8.4
83	14	2010	7.9
84	15	2011	7.4
85	16	2012	6.9
86	17	2013	6.5
87	18	2014	6.1
88	19	2015	5.7
89	20	2016	5.3
90	21	2017	5.0
91	22	2018	0.0

Question 7.4: *How did you arrive at the life expectancy of Marshall under the recalculation method for each of the distribution calendar years described in Question 7.3?*

Answer: Marshall must use the single life expectancy table under Table V of section 1.72–9 of the Income Tax Regulations. The single life expectancy of Marshall may also be found in Table I of IRS Publication 590, which is included in the Appendix of this book. The table shows a 16-year life expectancy for a 70-year-old person.

Marshall must use his single life expectancy because under the law the estate as his beneficiary has no life expectancy.

Question 7.5: *How does the single life expectancy table work if the recalculation method is used for Marshall and how does this compare to the term-certain method?*

Answer: If the recalculation method is used, then the life expectancy table must be consulted each year. Using his attained age as of his birthday in each year, Marshall's life expectancy changes each year by less than one. Under the recalculation method, Marshall's life expectancy is reduced to zero in the year following the year of his death.

Under the term-certain method, Marshall's life expectancy is reduced by one for each distribution calendar year that follows Marshall's first distribution calendar year. Thus, Marshall's term-certain period of 16 years for the first distribution year of 1997 would be reduced to 15 years for 1998, to 14 years for 1999, and so on until it is reduced to zero in the year 2013. In addition, the term-certain method survives Marshall's death should he die before the end of the term-certain period.

Question 7.6: *In Marshall's first distribution calendar year, is the required minimum distribution under the recalculation method less than under the term-certain method?*

Answer: No. Marshall's life expectancy is 16 years in his first distribution calendar year under both the term-certain method and recalculation method. The required minimum distribution under both methods is identical for the first distribution calendar year. There is no difference between the methods until the second distribution year.

Question 7.7: *How much must Marshall receive as his required minimum distribution for his first distribution calendar year 1997?*

Answer: Marshall must divide his single life expectancy of 16 years (Question 7.4) by his IRA account balance as of December 31, 1996, the end of the year preceding the first distribution calendar year 1997. Assuming that the account balance as of December 31, 1996 is $96,000, Marshall's required minimum distribution for the first distribution calendar year 1997 is $6,000.

Question 7.8: *Assume that Marshall received his $6,000 required minimum distribution for his first distribution calendar year 1997 on October 31, 1997. Further assume that his account balance in his IRA as of December 31, 1997 is $96,700. How much must Marshall receive during the second distribution calendar year 1998 under the recalculation method in order to satisfy the required minimum distribution rules for the calendar year 1998?*

Answer: $6,320.26. The calendar year 1998 is Marshall's second distribution calendar year. He must receive his required minimum distribution for his second distribution calendar year by December 31, 1998. In order to determine his required minimum distribution for the calendar year 1998, the value of his account balance as of December 31, 1997 must be divided by the appropriate life expectancy that is applicable to the calendar year 1998. The account balance of $96,700 is divided by 15.3 years, which is the life expectancy of Marshall under the recalculation method as of the second distribution calendar year 1998 as shown in the answer to Question 7.3. The result is $6,320.26.

Question 7.9: *Assume that Marshall has selected his estate as the beneficiary of his IRA. Marshall failed to elect the term-certain method by his required beginning date. The IRA plan document states that unless he elects out of the recalculation method by his required beginning date, he defaults into the recalculation method. Further assume that Marshall dies September 1, 2002 after receiving his required minimum distribution for the calendar year 2002. The calendar year 2002 is his sixth distribution calendar year. Assume that as of December 31, 2002 the account balance in Marshall's IRA is $100,000. What happens to Marshall's IRA in the calendar year 2003 under the recalculation method?*

Answer: The IRS requires that the IRA be liquidated and paid out in its entirety to Marshall's estate by no later than December 30, 2003. This payout would include any earnings on the $100,000 account balance in Marshall's IRA as well. Any losses would, of course, reduce the account balance.

Question 7.10: *Why does the entire account balance have to be paid to Marshall's estate by the end of the year following Marshall's death?*

Answer: Under the IRS rules, if Marshall is using the recalculation method, his life expectancy is reduced to zero in the calendar year following the calendar year of his death. The IRA institution must distribute Marshall's entire remaining interest in the account prior to the last day of 2003, the calendar year following the year of his death and the calendar year in which his life expectancy is reduced to zero.

Marshall's estate must receive the entire balance in Marshall's IRA during the period January 1, 2003 through December 30, 2003.

Question 7.11: *Assume that Marshall's estate receives all but $20,000 of Marshall's IRA during the period January 1, 2003 through December 30, 2003. The remaining $20,000 is received by the estate in the calendar year 2004. May the IRS assess a penalty against Marshall's estate?*

Answer: Yes. Marshall's estate received an insufficient distribution from Marshall's IRA during the calendar year 2003. The shortfall is $20,000. The IRS may assess a penalty of 50 percent of the shortfall of $20,000 or $10,000 against the estate for the calendar year 2003. Thus, Marshall's estate may be subject to a penalty of $10,000 for the calendar year 2003.

Question 7.12: *May the IRS waive the $10,000 penalty described in Question 7.11?*

Answer: Yes. The IRS may waive the penalty if the shortfall was due to reasonable error and reasonable steps are being taken to remedy the shortfall.

Question 7.13: *Should Marshall's estate select a calendar year for estate income tax purposes?*

Answer: No. If Marshall's estate uses a calendar year, then the entire balance in Marshall's IRA would be received in one taxable year of the estate.

Question 7.14: *Assume that Marshall died on September 1, 2002. What fiscal year could Marshall's estate elect?*

Answer: The executor of Marshall's estate could elect a fiscal year for the estate such as September 1, 2002 through August 31, 2003.

Question 7.15: *If Marshall's executor elected the fiscal year September 1, 2002 through August 31, 2003, may that election result in an overall income tax savings to the estate and/ or the heirs of the estate?*

Answer: Yes. Marshall's estate must receive Marshall's entire interest in his IRA between the period January 1, 2003 through December 30, 2003. If Marshall's estate has a fiscal year, then the IRA distribution from Marshall's IRA may be received in two fiscal years of the estate. A portion of Marshall's IRA may be received during the estate's fiscal year September 1, 2002 through August 31, 2003, and a portion of Marshall's IRA may be received during the estate's fiscal year September 1, 2003 through August 31, 2004. Remember that the entire interest of Marshall's IRA must be paid to Marshall's estate during the period January 1, 2003 through December 30, 2003. Allocating income over two fiscal years is generally worthwhile since it gives the executor and heirs an additional opportunity for tax planning. Income tax splitting and deferral of income tax liability is important in view of the high income tax rates that are currently applicable to estates and beneficiaries.

Question 7.16: *Assume that Marshall selected his estate as the beneficiary of his IRA. Prior to his required beginning date he timely elected to receive his required minimum distributions from his IRA over a 16-year term-certain period. Assume that Marshall died on September 1,*

2002 after receiving his required minimum distribution from his IRA for his sixth distribution calendar year 2002. Must Marshall's estate receive the entire interest from Marshall's IRA during the period January 1, 2003 through December 30, 2003?

Answer: No. Marshall's estate may receive the required minimum distributions from Marshall's IRA over the remaining 10 years that is left in the original 16-year term-certain period.

If an IRA owner timely elects a term-certain period and dies on or after his or her required beginning date, then the term-certain period may continue after the IRA owner's death. Since Marshall timely elected a 16-year term-certain period and died in his sixth distribution calendar year, his estate may receive required minimum distributions for the remaining 10-year period that is left in the initial 16-year term-certain period. In this situation, it does not matter that the estate is the beneficiary.

Question 7.17: *Based upon your answer to Question 7.16, must Marshall's estate receive the required minimum distributions from Marshall's IRA over the remaining 10-year period?*

Answer: No. Although the estate may not receive required minimum distributions over a period that exceeds the 10-year term-certain period, the executor may accelerate distributions from Marshall's IRA from time to time. The IRS asserts a 50% penalty when the recipient receives an insufficient distribution. No penalties apply if a distribution is greater than the required minimum distribution.

Question 7.18: *Assume that the executor of Marshall's estate does not wish to keep the estate open for 10 years. What action can the executor take other than accelerating distributions from Marshall's IRA?*

Answer: The executor may assign the remaining unpaid installments from Marshall's IRA to the beneficiaries of Marshall's estate. In that case, the beneficiaries may continue to receive the installments from Marshall's IRA over the balance of the term-certain period or accelerate distributions from time to time. However, before the installments are assigned to the beneficiaries of Marshall's estate, the IRA institution should be consulted. If the IRA institution refuses to go along with the assignment, then it may be necessary to obtain a letter ruling from the IRS in order to convince the IRA institution that the transaction is not in violation of any IRA rules.

Question 7.19: *Assume that Marshall's date of death is September 1, 2002. Upon the death of Marshall, how should his IRA account read to indicate that his estate is his beneficiary?*

Answer: The IRA account must be maintained in Marshall's name. It should read "Marshall Jones, deceased IRA (date of death: September 1, 2002), Estate of Marshall Jones, beneficiary ID No. 18-1000000." The failure to use the exact words described above should not prove fatal as long as the IRA account is maintained in Marshall's name.

Question 7.20: *Assume that Marshall's IRA account is erroneously changed after Marshall's death to read "Estate of Marshall Jones" and there is no reference to the words IRA in the account. What is the tax consequence of the change in the name of the account?*

Answer: The estate has a serious tax problem. The IRS will attempt to tax the entire account as a distribution of income to the estate. The IRA account must be maintained in Marshall's name in order to avoid a taxable event to the estate. If this situation should come up, then the estate should ask the financial institution to explain the error to the IRS. In the event that this explanation is not acceptable to the IRS, then the estate will have to litigate the tax issue with the IRS.

Question 7.21: *What is the advantage of Marshall's electing the 16-year term-certain period described above?*

Answer: In the event that Marshall dies during the 16-year term-certain period, then his estate can continue to use the balance of the term-certain period in order to receive the required minimum distributions from Marshall's IRA. This is especially beneficial if Marshall should die during the first half of the term-certain period.

Question 7.22: *What is the advantage of Marshall using the recalculation method of receiving required minimum distributions from his IRA?*

Answer: If Marshall lives beyond age 85, he will still be able to continue to receive required minimum distributions from his IRA; see the recalculation table accompanying Question 7.3. This assumes that Marshall has not withdrawn all of his money from his IRA at an earlier point in time.

Question 7.23: *Assume that Marshall selected his estate as the beneficiary of his IRA. What is the disadvantage of Marshall's using the recalculation method of receiving required minimum distributions from his IRA?*

Answer: If Marshall should die at a point in time when he has a substantial amount of assets in his IRA, then the entire interest in his IRA must be paid out between January 1 and December 30 of the calendar year following the calendar year of his death. This will result in an acceleration of income and the loss of the tax deferred growth of his IRA account.

Question 7.24: *Which approach should Marshall select—the term-certain method or the recalculation method?*

Answer: There is no easy answer. If Marshall is conservative and wishes to protect the heirs to his estate, then he should use the term-certain method. If he is a gambler and wishes to bet on a long life and is not concerned with the potential income acceleration problem that is attendant with the recalculation method, then he should use the recalculation method. Marshall should be told about the pros and cons of each method and should make the ultimate decision.

Account Owner Dies Before the Required Beginning Date:

The following questions and answers discuss the special distribution rules that apply to your estate, as your beneficiary, if you die before your required beginning date.

Question 7.25: *Assume that John Rogers, an employee of XYZ Corporation, is a participant in the corporation's qualified retirement plan. John, who is unmarried, dies at age 69 on July 1, 1996, leaving his qualified plan death benefits payable to his estate. What are the IRS distribution rules that are applicable to the qualified plan death benefits?*

Answer: The required beginning date for receiving required minimum distributions is April 1 of the calendar year following the calendar year in which the plan participant attains age 70 $1/2$. There are special rules if someone dies before the April 1 required beginning date. John died at age 69 before his required beginning date. The distribution rules that are applicable depend on who is going to receive the qualified plan death benefits. In this case the death benefits are payable to an estate. If John dies before his required beginning date and the estate is the beneficiary, then the estate must receive the qualified plan death benefits based upon a five-year rule. Thus, if John died at age 69 on July 1, 1996, then according to the Internal Revenue Code the estate must receive the entire distribution within five years from his date of death. This would bring the date of distribution of the death benefits to June 30, 2001. However, the IRS has administratively extended the date to December 31 of the calendar year that contains the fifth anniversary of the plan participant's date of death. Thus, the estate could receive the qualified plan death benefits by no later than December 31, 2001.

The IRS has issued several private letter rulings that indicate that if the estate is a conduit for payments to the surviving spouse of the plan participant, then the five-year may not be applicable. Since John was not married, this "conduit" exception has no application here.

Question 7.26: *May partial distributions be made to John's estate during the period between July 1, 1996 and December 31, 2001?*

Answer: Yes. The IRS rules set the outer limits for the timing of the payments of the qualified death benefits to the estate if the plan participant dies before his required beginning date. However, for tax-planning purposes, partial distributions of the qualified plan death benefits may be made to the estate during the following periods:

July 1, 1996 to December 31, 1996

January 1, 1997 to December 31, 1997

January 1, 1998 to December 31, 1998

January 1, 1999 to December 31, 1999

January 1, 2000 to December 31, 2000

January 1, 2001 to December 31, 2001

Question 7.27: *Why would the estate want to receive partial distributions rather than withdrawing the full amount immediately?*

Answer: The longer the funds stay in the qualified plan, the greater the tax-deferred growth. In addition, significant tax planning can take place if a longer period of deferral is available.

Question 7.28: *I was informed that estates were placed in a high income tax bracket by the 1993 tax act. Therefore, what is the value of deferring income only to have it paid to the estate and taxed at a high income tax bracket?*

Answer: Through proper tax planning you can avoid the high income tax bracket that is applicable to an estate under the 1993 tax act. The 1993 tax act quickly moves estate taxable income into the 36% bracket. For example, under the 1995 tax rate schedules, the 36% bracket applies to an estate with taxable income in excess of $5,600 and the 39.6% bracket applies if estate taxable income exceeds $7,650. The $5,600 and $7,650 amounts are adjusted annually for inflation.

These high income tax rates can be avoided. One of several approaches that can be used is to elect a fiscal year for the estate and to make timely distributions to the beneficiaries. In this way the taxable income is shifted to the beneficiaries whose individual income tax brackets are generally not as high as the estate income tax brackets.

Question 7.29: *What happens if the final distribution of the qualified plan death benefits in the amount of $100,000 is not made to John's estate until after December 31, 2001?*

Answer: The IRS can penalize both the plan and the estate.

Question 7.30: *What type of tax liability can the IRS assess against the plan?*

Answer: The IRS can penalize the plan for violating the required minimum distribution rules. The amount of penalty is negotiable and is based upon the degree of negligence of the plan administrator.

Question 7.31: *What type of penalty can be assessed against the estate?*

Answer: The penalty against the estate can be significant. The Internal Revenue Code provides for a penalty of 50% of the shortfall in the distribution, which in this case amounts to $50,000 (50% × $100,000). However, the IRS states that the penalty may be waived if the shortfall is due to a reasonable error and reasonable steps are taken to correct the shortfall.

Question 7.32: *John has been told that he may select his son, Richard, as the designated beneficiary of his qualified plan benefits instead of his estate. Is there an advantage if he selects his son as the designated beneficiary?*

Answer: Yes. If he selects his son as the designated beneficiary of his retirement assets, then the distribution options that are available to his son are significantly different from the options that are available to John's estate. These options are discussed in other chapters of this book.

Question 7.33: *Why is there a difference in the distribution rules when a designated beneficiary is involved?*

Answer: The IRS rules are quite liberal when it comes to paying death benefits to a designated beneficiary instead of an estate.

Question 7.34: *Is an estate considered to be a designated beneficiary?*

Answer: No. An estate is considered to be a beneficiary, not a designated beneficiary. Only an individual may be a designated beneficiary. In addition, an individual who receives retirement distributions under an irrevocable trust is considered to be a designated beneficiary as well. Where the account owner dies before the required beginning date, then death benefits to a designated beneficiary may be paid over the designated beneficiary's single life expectancy if the appropriate timely election is made. Death benefits to an estate must be paid under the five-year rule as explained in the answer to Question 7.25 if death takes place before the required begining date.

CHAPTER 8

Death Benefit Rules for Your Nonspouse Designated Beneficiaries

The IRS retirement distribution rules affect not only your lifetime payments from IRAs and qualified plans but also the timing and amount of distributions that will be made to your designated beneficiaries after your death. Different rules will apply to your designated beneficiaries depending on your age when you die, and, in some cases, upon who the designated beneficiary is.

If you have reached age 70¹/₂, and have begun to take required minimum distributions from your account, then generally, after your death, your designated beneficiary must follow the same method you were using in order to calculate the amount that he or she must receive as required minimum distributions. The specific application of these designated beneficiary rules is discussed throughout this book in the relevant chapters. For example, the distribution rules for spousal beneficiaries are in Chapter 3, for designated beneficiaries more than 10 years younger in Chapter 4, and for other adult beneficiaries in Chapter 6.

In this chapter we will cover the special distribution rules that apply to nonspouse designated beneficiaries where the IRA owner or plan participant dies before his or her required beginning date; that is, before April 1 of the calendar year following the calendar year in which he or she would have reached age 70¹/₂. The spousal rules were discussed in Chapter 3.

Designated Beneficiary Basics:

The following questions and answers provide an introduction to the distribution rules for designated beneficiaries.

Question 8.1: *Do the IRS rules for distributions to designated beneficiaries apply to corporate retirement plans as well as IRAs?*

Answer: Yes. Distributions from the following types of retirement plans are subject to the designated beneficiary rules:

a. Individual retirement plans such as an Individual Retirement Account or an Individual Retirement Annuity;

b. Annuity contracts under IRC Sec. 403(b);

c. Qualified plans of a corporation or self-employed employer, such as a pension plan, profit sharing plan, or stock bonus plan;

d. Qualified annuity plans under IRC Sec. 403(a); and

e. Simplified employee pensions.

Question 8.2: *What distribution options will my designated beneficiaries have after my death?*

Answer: Different distribution options apply depending on whether or not the date of death is before your required beginning date. The required beginning date is April 1 of the calendar year following the year in which you attain age $70^1/_2$. Certain exceptions were previously discussed in this book. See Chapter 2, Question 2.3.

If the date of death is on or after the required beginning date, then your designated beneficiary's options generally depend on whether your required minimum distributions were being determined under the term-certain or recalculation method. These rules were discussed in the previous chapters of this book.

If the date of death is before the required beginning date, then your designated beneficiary may be able to choose under the IRS rules between receiving distributions from your account over a five-year period or over his or her life expectancy. However, the terms of your plan must be followed. If your plan document is not as liberal as the IRS rules, then the IRS requires the more restrictive plan rules to be followed.

Special averaging may be available to a beneficiary or a designated beneficiary for a lump-sum distribution from a qualified employer plan.

Question 8.3: *Does that mean that if under the IRS rules my designated beneficiary can receive distributions over his or her life expectancy, which happens to be 40 years, but the plan limits the distribution period to 20 years, my designated beneficiary loses 20 years of tax-deferred growth?*

Answer: Yes. The IRS requires the plan document provisions to be followed. The plan document provisions may be stricter than the IRS distribution payment rules. The administrator of your plan may not wish to be burdened with the responsibility of paying out distributions to a designated beneficiary over a 40-year period, even though that period does not exceed the designated beneficiary's life expectancy. Many company plans that have been approved by the IRS limit the payout period to 20 years.

Question 8.4: *Can the plan document provide that distributions can be made over a greater than the IRS permits?*

Answer: No. It would be illegal for the plan document to provide that distributions can be made over a greater period than that permitted under the IRS rules, which follow the guidelines spelled out by Congress in the Internal Revenue Code.

Question 8.5: *Assume that my son has been properly designated as my designated beneficiary under a corporate qualified plan. Is there anything I can do to take advantage of the longer payment rules that are available to my son as my designated beneficiary if my current plan has a restricted payout period that is not as good as the maximum IRS payout period?*

Answer: Yes. Speak to your employer and ask him to consider amending the plan to provide for increased payout flexibility in the event of your death. If your employer states that it is too difficult or that it would be an administrative nightmare to create a sophisticated distribution payout arrangement, then you have a problem. In this case, your employer's plan is preventing your son from taking advantage of the extended payout period that the IRS would otherwise allow to your son as your designated beneficiary.

Question 8.6: *Assume that the employer refuses to amend the plan to increase the period over which distributions can be paid. Is there any other solution to resolve this problem?*

Answer: You should point out to the president of the company that many employees are affected by the payout option and that perhaps the employer should amend the plan to provide that any employee who has attained retirement age in the plan may receive a within service plan distribution although continuing to work for the employer. Such a within service plan distribution would permit the individual plan participant to transfer the value of his or her benefits in the plan directly to an Individual Retirement Account that has liberal payout options. Naturally the necessary paperwork and spousal consents, where required, would have to be obtained. This amendment would be valuable to the key employees of the corporation as well as to the rank and file employees and should not be unduly burdensome to the plan administrator.

Question 8.7: *Is there any other approach that can be used?*

Answer: Yes. If the employer is still not interested in amending the plan to provide for either a liberalization of the payout terms or refuses to provide for a within service plan distribution, then if the stakes are high enough you might consider separating from service. Many plans provide for a lump-sum distribution upon separation from service. If you are contemplating retirement or leaving the company, then examine the plan document in order to determine whether you are entitled to a lump-sum distribution upon termination of employment.

Question 8.8: *What happens if the plan document distribution rules are based upon an old plan document that does not conform with the current IRS rules?*

Answer: The plan document must conform with the IRS distribution rules. The IRS rules override any distribution options in the plan that are inconsistent with current law.

The Five-Year Rule and Life Expectancy Rule:

The following questions and answers illustrate the basic five-year distribution rule, and the life expectancy exception rule, that may be available to designated beneficiaries of plan participants who die before the required beginning date.

Question 8.9: *John Smyth is the sole owner of a corporation and has accumulated $1,000,000 in his qualified profit sharing plan. John is the only participant in the qualified plan and has no intention of hiring any new employees, other than his son, Richard. Richard is his only child and his sole beneficiary. John's wife passed away last year. John dies on July 1, 1997 at the age of 69. Richard is age 40 in 1997. What distribution options are available to Richard?*

Answer: If John dies at the age of 69, before his required beginning date, then Richard, as John's designated beneficiary, may have a choice of options under the terms of the plan document as to when he must commence distributions from the plan. These options may include the following:

a. The entire distribution must be received by Richard by December 31 of the fifth year following the year of John's date of death; or

b. Payments may be paid over Richard's life or over a period not extending beyond Richard's life expectancy.

Question 8.10: *Are the two options described above always available to Richard?*

Answer: No. The plan document may provide that only one option applies, or the plan may permit Richard as the designated beneficiary to elect which rule applies. In addition, if the plan document is silent, or if no election is made by Richard, then the five-year rule is automatically applicable. This automatic five-year rule applies only where the designated beneficiary is someone other than a surviving spouse.

Question 8.11: *If the plan document permits the designated beneficiary to make the election as to which method to use, how is the election made?*

Answer: The IRS does not indicate the mechanics of making the election. However, if the designated beneficiary is not a surviving spouse, then the election into the life expectancy rule must be made by no later than December 31 of the year following the year of the plan participant's date of death. In addition, payments must commence by that December 31 date as well. The election must be irrevocable.

Question 8.12: *How is the election described above made by Richard if he wishes to avoid the five-year rule?*

Answer: The IRS rules do not describe the form of the election or where to file the election. Obviously, the election must be in writing in order to prove to the IRS that it was timely made. If the election is not timely made, then the five-year rule becomes operative. Richard must make a timely written election with the plan administrator by no later than December 31 of the year following the year in which his father passed away and must commence distributions by that date as well. The election must be irrevocable.

Richard should make a timely written election with the plan administrator of the qualified profit sharing plan electing to receive the required minimum distributions from the qualified plan over a period of years that does not exceed his life expectancy as determined under the IRS life expectancy tables. Once again it is possible that the plan does not permit the payments to be made over a period that is tied into Richard's life expectancy. The plan may have an arbitrary cutoff period of perhaps 20 years or less.

Question 8.13: *Specifically, if John dies on July 1, 1997, before his required beginning date, what must Richard do in order to elect out of the five-year rule?*

Answer: Richard must do the following:

a. He must elect in writing by no later than December 31, 1998 that he wishes to elect out of the five-year rule. The deadline of December 31, 1998 is the end of the year following the year (1997) in which his father died.

b. He must elect in writing that he wishes to receive his required minimum distributions from the profit sharing plan based upon a term-certain period that does not exceed his life expectancy. It is best that the term-certain period be indicated in the written election form filed with the plan administrator. The failure to indicate the term-certain period should not prove fatal.

c. That term-certain period is based upon the life expectancy of Richard. The life expectancy of Richard is based upon IRS life expectancy tables. The life expectancy that is used is the IRS life expectancy of Richard as determined in the calendar year 1998, the year following the year of John's death. Since Richard is age 40 in 1997, the year of his father's death, his attained age in 1998 is 41. The life expectancy at age 41 is 41.5 years, as shown in Table I of the Appendix of this book.

d. The written election must be served upon the plan administrator of the qualified profit sharing plan by no later than December 31, 1998. This written election should be sent by certified mail, return receipt requested, to prove the timeliness of the election.

e. The written election should state that this election to receive required minimum distributions over a term-certain period of 41.5 years is irrevocable with respect to Richard and all subsequent beneficiaries. This, of course, assumes that the qualified profit sharing plan does not limit the distribution period to a lesser period of perhaps 20 years.

f. The written election should state that Richard may accelerate payments from time to time during the term-certain period that he elected.

g. The written election should cover additional contingencies. For example, it should specify what happens to the remaining payments if Richard dies during the payout period.

h. In order for the exception to the five-year rule to be operative, the first required minimum distribution to Richard must be received from the qualified profit-sharing plan by no later than December 31, 1998.

Question 8.14: *Assume that John's account balance at his date of death on July 1, 1997 is $1,000,000. The plan year of the qualified profit sharing plan is a calendar year. On December 31, 1997, his account balance is $1,050,000. Also assume that under the terms of the plan, Richard may receive the $1,050,000 of death benefits from the qualified profit sharing plan over a 20-year term-certain period in equal, annual installments. This is accomplished by the plan trustees purchasing a 20-year term-certain annuity contract with an insurance company. Assume that the annual installments are based upon a 7% interest assumption. How much money will Richard receive over a 20-year term-certain period based upon equal, annual installment payments?*

Answer: Richard will receive equal annual payments of $99,112.57 for a period of 20 years for a total distribution of $1,982,251.40.

Question 8.15: *Assume that Richard may receive the $1,050,000 of death benefits from the qualified profit sharing plan over a 20-year period based upon the required minimum distribution rules, instead of under an annuity contract as in Question 8.14. Assume that the required minimum distributions are based upon a 7% interest assumption. How much money will Richard receive over the 20-year period based upon the required minimum distribution rules?*

Answer: Richard will receive total required minimum distributions over the 20-year period of $2,361,224.28. The following schedule illustrates the computation of the required minimum distribution over a 20-year period.

Initial amount: $1,050,000.00, Earnings: 7%

Distributions over 20 years

Year	Earnings at 7%	Required Minimum Distributions	Balance
			$1,050,000.00
1	$ 73,500.00	$ 52,500.00	1,071,000.00
2	74,970.00	56,368.42	1,089,601.58
3	76,272.11	60,533.42	1,105,340.27
4	77,373.82	65,020.02	1,117,694.07
5	78,238.58	69,855.88	1,126,076.77
6	78,825.37	75,071.78	1,129,830.36
7	79,088.13	80,702.17	1,128,216.32
8	78,975.14	86,785.87	1,120,405.59
9	78,428.39	93,367.13	1,105,466.85
10	77,382.68	100,496.99	1,082,352.54
11	75,764.68	108,235.25	1,049,881.97
12	73,491.74	116,653.55	1,006,720.16
13	70,470.41	125,840.02	951,350.55
14	66,594.54	135,907.22	882,037.87
15	61,742.65	147,006.31	796,774.21
16	55,774.19	159,354.84	693,193.56

cont'd

(continued from previous page)

Year	Earnings at 7%	Required Minimum Distributions	Balance
17	48,523.55	173,298.39	568,418.72
18	39,789.31	189,472.91	418,735.12
19	29,311.46	209,367.56	238,679.02
20	16,707.53	255,386.55	0.00
	$1,311,224.28	$2,361,224.28	

Question 8.16: *Assume that under the terms of John's plan Richard may receive the $1,050,000 of death benefits from the qualified profit sharing plan over a 41- (41.5-year life expectancy rounded down to 41 years for illustrative purposes) year term-certain period in equal, annual installments. This is accomplished by the plan trustees purchasing a 41-year term-certain annuity contract with an insurance company. Assume that the annual installments are based upon a 7% interest assumption. How much money will Richard receive over a 41-year period based upon equal annual installment payments?*

Answer: Richard will receive equal, annual payments of $78,392.61 for a period of 41 years for a total distribution of $3,214,097.01.

Question 8.17: *Assume that Richard may receive the $1,050,000 of death benefits from the qualified profit sharing plan over a 41- (41.5 years rounded down to 41 years for illustrative purposes) year period based upon the required minimum distribution rules, instead of under an annuity contract as in Question 8.16. Assume that the required minimum distribution rules are based upon a 7% interest assumption. How much money will Richard receive over the 41-year period based upon the required minimum distribution rules?*

Answer: Richard will receive total required minimum distributions over the 41-year period of $6,180,876.46. The following schedule illustrates the computation of the required minimum distribution over a 41-year period.

Initial amount: $1,050,000.00, Earnings: 7%

Distributions over 41 years

Year	Earnings at 7%	Required Minimum Distributions	Balance
			$1,050,000.00
1	$ 73,500.00	$ 25,609.76	1,097,890.24
2	76,852.32	27,447.26	1,147,295.30
3	80,310.67	29,417.83	1,198,188.14
4	83,873.17	31,531.27	1,250,530.04
5	87,537.10	33,798.11	1,304,269.03
6	91,298.83	36,229.70	1,359,338.16

cont'd

(continued from previous page)

Year	Earnings at 7%	Required Minimum Distributions	Balance
7	95,153.67	38,838.23	1,415,653.60
8	99,095.75	41,636.87	1,473,112.48
9	103,117.87	44,639.77	1,531,590.58
10	107,211.34	47,862.21	1,590,939.71
11	111,365.78	51,320.64	1,650,984.85
12	115,568.94	55,032.83	1,711.520.96
13	119,806.47	59,017.96	1,772,309.47
14	124,061.66	63,296.77	1,833,074.36
15	128,315.21	67,891.64	1,893,497.93
16	132,544.86	72,826.84	1,953,215.95
17	136,725.12	78,128.64	2,011,812.43
18	140,826.87	83,825.52	2,068,813.78
19	144,816.96	89,948.43	2,123,682.31
20	148,657.76	96,531.01	2,175,809.06
21	152,306.63	103,609.96	2,224,505.73
22	155,715.40	111,225.29	2,268,995.84
23	158,829.71	119,420.83	2,308,404.72
24	161,588.33	128,244.71	2,341,748.34
25	163,922.38	137,749.90	2,367,920.82
26	165,754.46	147,995.05	2,385,680.23
27	166,997.62	159,045.35	2,393,632.50
28	167,554.28	170,973.75	2,390,213.03
29	167,314.91	183,862.54	2,373,665.40
30	166,156.58	197,805.45	2,342,016.53
31	163,941.16	212,910.59	2,293,047.10
32	160,513.30	229,304.71	2,224.255.69
33	155,697.90	247,139.52	2,132,814.07
34	149,296.98	266,601.76	2,015,509.29
35	141,085.65	287,929.90	1,868,665.04
36	130,806.55	311,444.17	1,688,027.42
37	118,161.92	337,605.48	1,468,583.86
38	102,800.87	367,145.96	1,204,238.77
39	84,296.71	401,412.92	887,122.56
40	62,098.58	443,561.28	505,659.86
41	35,396.19	541,056.05	0.00
	$5,130,876.46	$6,180,876.46	

Question 8.18: *Under the facts of Question 8.17, how is Richard's required minimum distribution for 1998 determined?*

Answer: The account balance as of the end of the plan year in which John died is used in the calculation together with Richard's life expectancy. Richard's life expectancy is determined in the calendar year 1998 and is based upon the IRS single life expectancy tables. John died on July 1, 1997. The plan year is a calendar year and therefore the decedent's account balance as of December 31, 1997 must be used. The account balance as of December 31, 1997 is $1,050,000. The IRS life expectancy of Richard in 1998, the year following John's date of death, is 41.5 years. The account balance of $1,050,000 is divided by 41.5 years in order to determine Richard's required minimum distribution for the calendar year 1998. Richard's required minimum distribution for 1998 is therefore $25,301.20 ($1,050,000 ÷ 41.5 years). The schedule in the answer to Question 8.17 shows a slightly higher total than this because a 41-year period (rather than 41.5) was used in the schedule for illustrative purposes.

Question 8.19: *May Richard receive an amount in excess of $25,301.20 from the qualified plan during the calendar year 1998?*

Answer: Yes. $25,301.20 is the required minimum distribution that Richard must receive from the qualified profit-sharing plan in order to satisfy the law and avoid an IRS penalty. He can receive an amount in excess of $25,301.20 without any penalty. This assumes that the plan permits the acceleration of distributions from time to time.

Question 8.20: *Since Richard must continue to receive required minimum distributions in subsequent years as well, how much must he receive during the calendar year 1999?*

Answer: Richard must receive a required minimum distribution for the calendar year 1999, which is equal to the decedent's account balance as of December 31, 1998, divided by the remaining years that are left in Richard's life expectancy.

Question 8.21: *If we assume that the account balance as of December 31, 1998 is $1,075,000, then how much must Richard receive as a required minimum distribution in 1999?*

Answer: Richard must receive a required minimum distribution of $26,543.21 from the qualified plan for the calendar year 1999. This is calculated by dividing the decedent's account balance of $1,075,000 as of December 31, 1998 by 40.5 years.

Question 8.22: *Why is 40.5 years used in calculating the required minimum distribution for Richard for the calendar year 1999?*

Answer: Richard's life expectancy is required to be reduced by one for each calendar year after 1998. The first year for which Richard had to receive a required minimum distribution is the calendar year 1998.

Question 8.23: *How would Richard's required minimum distribution from the qualified plan be calculated for the calendar year 2000?*

Answer: The decedent's account balance as of December 31, 1999 would be divided by 39.5 years. The required minimum distribution to Richard (assuming a reasonable rate of return) should increase each year.

Question 8.24: *Must Richard continue to receive his required minimum distributions from the qualified plan for the balance of the 41.5-year period?*

Answer: No. If he decides to take out the entire balance in the qualified plan in a given year, then his required minimum distributions in the subsequent years would be zero. Given the large account balance, Richard would incur a substantial tax liability in withdrawing the balance in one year or even over several years, and should take this into account in consultation with his tax advisor. This assumes that the qualified plan permits the acceleration of distributions from time to time.

Question 8.25: *Assume that Richard is required to receive a required minimum distribution of $40,000 in a given year, but only receives $30,000 for that calendar year. What penalty may the IRS assess against Richard?*

Answer: The IRS may assess a 50% penalty on the shortfall distribution. On a shortfall of $10,000, the penalty is $5,000. However, the penalty of $5,000 may be abated if Richard can explain the reason for the discrepancy to the IRS.

Question 8.26: *If Richard wishes to withdraw $50,000 from the qualified plan in a given year when he is only required to withdraw $40,000, may he receive a credit for this extra $10,000 against a subsequent year's required minimum distribution?*

Answer: No. The IRS does not permit a credit to be taken if a designated beneficiary receives a distribution in excess of his required minimum distribution. The extra money Richard took will have an indirect effect on his required minimum distributions in subsequent years. This is because the decedent's account balance has been reduced by the extra $10,000 withdrawal and the reduced account balance is used in order to determine the required minimum distribution for subsequent calendar years.

Question 8.27: *Since Richard is under the age of 59½ at the time he starts to receive the required minimum distributions from the qualified plan, is he subject to the 10% penalty on early distributions?*

Answer: No. The law provides that certain distributions are not subject to the 10% early distribution penalty. One of the exceptions to the 10% penalty is payments that are made to a designated beneficiary or a beneficiary upon the death of the plan participant. Richard can receive without penalty death benefits from the qualified plan and it does not matter whether he as the designated beneficiary is over or under age $59^1/_2$ at the date of the plan participant's death.

Question 8.28: *Assume that John had selected his estate as his beneficiary instead of Richard. If John died at age 55, would the estate be subject to the 10% early distribution penalty?*

Answer: No. Distributions of death benefits from a qualified plan are not subject to the 10% additional tax on early distributions. It does not matter whether the decedent at the date of his death was under or over age $59^1/_2$. Furthermore, it makes no difference whether a designated beneficiary (Richard) or a beneficiary (estate) receives the death benefits from a qualified plan. The estate has no life expectancy and as beneficiary would have to receive the entire account balance under the five-year rule.

Question 8.29: *Richard would like to know whether he can roll over the qualified plan death benefits into an Individual Retirement Account (IRA). Can he make such a rollover?*

Answer: No. If the designated beneficiary is not a surviving spouse, then he or she cannot rollover the plan death benefits into an IRA. (There was an exception to this rule for those participants who died before January 1, 1984.)

Question 8.30: *Will there be any problems for the profit sharing plan if Richard withdraws the plan death benefits over a period that does not exceed his 41.5-year life expectancy?*

Answer: Perhaps. The IRS has indicated that the qualified plan must be an active plan and not a wasting trust. Richard must therefore continue the profit sharing plan and make employer contributions to the plan from time to time in order to have an active plan.

Question 8.31: *Should Richard take over his father's corporation and keep the plan active?*

Answer: Perhaps. Richard may not be interested in maintaining his father's corporation. Richard may have no interest in his father's business or in maintaining the corporation for a 41.5-year period.

Question 8.32: *What may the IRS do if Richard refuses to keep his father's corporation active?*

Answer: The IRS has indicated that the tax exempt status of a trust that is maintained by the plan may be revoked if the plan is not an active plan.

Question 8.33: *What is the effect of an IRS revocation of the trust's tax exempt status?*

Answer: If the trust's tax exempt status is revoked, then all the earnings in the trust become taxable to the trust each year.

Question 8.34: *Assume that Richard receives a $30,000 distribution of plan death benefits in 1999. What happens if the plan assets earn ordinary income of $50,000 in 1999 and the IRS on audit retroactively revokes the plan's tax exempt status for that year?*

Answer: The IRS will assess an income tax liability against the trust. The income tax liability is computed as follows:

Income from trust		$50,000
Less: Distribution to Richard	$30,000	
Trust exemption	100	30,100
Taxable income		$19,900

The income tax liability for 1999 can only be approximated, using the following 1995 tax rates (the latest available) as a guide. The actual rate brackets for 1999 will be different because of inflation adjustments. In 1995, the rates for a trust were as follows:

15% on first $1,550 of taxable income

28% on taxable income between $1,550 and $3,700

31% on taxable income between $3,700 and $5,600

36% on taxable income between $5,600 and $7,650

39.6% on taxable income in excess of $7,650

Based on the above rate schedule, the income tax liability on $19,900 would be $7,012.50. As a result of inflation adjustments to the above 1995 brackets, the actual liability for 1999 should be somewhat lower. The IRS will assess interest and penalties as well.

Question 8.35: *If the IRS revokes the tax exempt status of the plan's trust what course of action is available to the employer?*

Answer: The employer may appeal the IRS determination and try to resolve the dispute within the IRS or litigate the issue in the United States Tax Court or any other federal court.

Question 8.36: *Is there any option that is available to the plan trustees?*

Answer: Yes. The plan trustees may invest the plan assets in tax exempt investments and therefore avoid having a trust income tax liability in the future.

Question 8.37: *Is there anything that Richard may do in order to avoid the trust income tax liability in the future?*

Answer: Yes. He may withdraw all of the trust earnings each year so that the trust will have no taxable income in the future.

Question 8.38: *What can John do while he is alive in order to protect Richard from a dispute with the IRS?*

Answer: John can arrange for the termination of the qualified profit sharing plan and the transfer of his interest in the qualified profit sharing plan directly to a brand new IRA. If John is married, then he must obtain spousal consent in order to make the transfer to the IRA. He can then select Richard as the designated beneficiary of his IRA. If this is done, then all of the options and elections that were available to Richard as the designated beneficiary of a plan participant are available to Richard as the designated beneficiary of John's IRA. All the potential problems of maintaining a qualified plan for the 41.5-year period can then be avoided.

Question 8.39: *If John dies on July 1, 1997 at age 69 and the qualified profit-sharing assets have previously been transferred to an IRA, then what must Richard do in order to be able to receive distributions over his life expectancy?*

Answer: Assuming that the terms of the IRA require an election to avoid the five-year method, Richard must make such an election, in writing, with the IRA institution by no later than December 31 of the calendar year following the year in which John died. Richard must commence his required minimum distributions by that date as well. The written election must be irrevocable and should be mailed certified return receipt requested to the IRA institution. The written election should contain the same information that was previously described in the answer to Question 8.13, when Richard made the election as the designated beneficiary of John's profit sharing plan. The same required minimum distribution rules that applied to Richard on the extended payout period of 41.5 years from the qualified plan apply to the required minimum distributions from the IRA except that IRA distribution options have greater flexibility than qualified plan payout options.

Question 8.40: *What other reason is there to have John transfer his qualified plan assets directly to an IRA before his death?*

Answer: Qualified plans are required to file annual reports with the Internal Revenue Service. This requirement is not applicable to IRAs. In addition, the Internal Revenue Code is frequently amended and employers are burdened with the responsibility and cost of amending plans to conform with the changes in the law and regulations. In addition, qualified plans are subject to audit by the IRS. If Richard is not interested in taking over John's corporation then the plan should be terminated, if possible, prior to John's death. The plan assets should then be immediately transferred to a new IRA in John's name. If Richard is interested in taking over John's business but is not interested in maintaining the plan for an extended period of time, then the plan should be terminated prior to John's death and the plan assets should be transferred to John's new IRA.

Question 8.41: *Can John transfer his qualified plan assets to an IRA without the necessity of terminating the plan?*

Answer: Yes. A plan can be amended to provide that a participant may receive a distribution from the plan on or after reaching retirement age regardless of whether the participant separates from service with the employer. If the plan has the above provision and John has attained his retirement age as stated in the plan document, then he can receive his then existing account balance and transfer it directly to his new IRA. At least the bulk of his account balance will be in a new IRA. This does not prevent John from having further employer contributions made to the profit sharing plan on his behalf. To prevent withholding, John should make a "direct rollover" from the plan to the IRA, instead of actually receiving payment from the plan and then making the rollover; see Question 1.15.

Question 8.42: *If John transferred his qualified plan assets directly to an IRA, would Richard have greater investment control over the assets than if they had remained in the corporate plan?*

Answer: Perhaps. Richard could maintain control of the investments made by the IRA. He could not, however, control the investments made by the plan trustees of the corporate plan unless he was also a plan trustee. Assume that Richard is not a plan trustee and that he is receiving a 41.5-year payout from the qualified corporate plan. He will be unable during the 41.5-year payout period to prevent the trustees from making unwise investments or from committing improper transactions. To the extent that the plan permits, Richard may wish to accelerate distributions from the qualified plan in order to avoid the anxiety over what might happen to the corporate plan assets over the 41.5-year payout period.

Beneficiary's Death During Payout Period:

The following questions and answers illustrate the distribution rules that apply following the death of a designated beneficiary who has begun to receive required minimum distributions.

Question 8.43: *Could Richard during his lifetime direct the plan administrator or IRA custodian to pay upon his death the remaining unpaid installments directly to certain beneficiaries without the necessity of going though his estate?*

Answer: Probably yes. There is nothing in the tax law that prohibits Richard from designating beneficiaries of the remaining unpaid installments of the qualified plan death benefits or the IRA death benefits that are attributable to John. The right to designate the successor beneficiary of Richard's rights in the event of his death after John is a matter of state law. Richard should generally be able to select a successor beneficiary of the unpaid installments. If he does not have that right, or he does but fails to select a successor beneficiary, the remaining qualified plan or IRA installments would be payable to his estate.

Question 8.44: *Are there any advantages in having the unpaid installments of the qualified plan death benefits or IRA death benefits to which Richard is entitled payable to his estate upon his death?*

Answer: Yes. The estate can use a fiscal year instead of a calendar year and this can result in certain tax deferral techniques. In addition, if there is an estate tax liquidity problem, then the executor may generally accelerate distributions in order to have assets available to pay the estate taxes and other administration expenses. The qualified plan provisions would have to be consulted in order to determine whether the executor may accelerate distributions from time to time. IRA death benefits may generally be accelerated at will.

Question 8.45: *Are there any other advantages in having the estate of Richard as the beneficiary of any unpaid installments of John's qualified plan death benefits or IRA death benefits?*

Answer: Yes. If the ultimate beneficiaries of Richard's estate are not prudent investors or are relatively young and inexperienced or would tend to make unwise decisions that would cause the assets to be dissipated, then it is best that the executor have control over the option to accelerate the death benefit distributions for a period of time.

Question 8.46: *If Richard dies during the 41.5-year payout period while receiving payments from John's IRA and the remaining installments are paid to his estate, must his estate be kept open for the balance of Richard's 41.5-year payout period?*

Answer: No. Richard's estate can continue to receive the remaining installment payments or may accelerate the payments from time to time if the IRA payment option provisions do not prohibit such acceleration. The estate steps into Richard's payment options. Under state law, the estate may generally assign the remaining installments to the beneficiaries of Richard's estate.

Question 8.47: *If the executor of Richard's estate assigns the remaining installments to the beneficiaries of Richard's estate, what options are available to the beneficiaries?*

Answer: The beneficiaries could continue to receive the remaining installments over the installment period, or they may accelerate the distributions from time to time if the payment option provisions do not prohibit such acceleration.

Question 8.48: *If Richard's estate has two beneficiaries, how should the installments be assigned?*

Answer: The executor should assign to each beneficiary a 50% interest in the rights to the installment payments from the qualified plan or IRA. The plan administrator or IRA institution should be notified as to the assignment of these installment rights.

Question 8.49: *Why is it best for Richard's estate to assign the installment rights to the beneficiaries of Richard's estate?*

Answer: It relieves the executor of Richard's estate from the problem of leaving the estate open for many years. The executor may wish to have an informal or formal discharge from fiduciary liability and would not be able to obtain this discharge for many years if he continues to receive installments over a long period of time. In addition, the executor will have to file tax returns and maintain a set of books for the period that the estate is maintained. This may be costly and burdensome.

Question 8.50: *Is there any other reason that the executor should assign the installment rights to the beneficiaries of the estate?*

Answer: Yes. If the executor assigns the rights to the future installments of the retirement assets proportionately to each beneficiary of the estate, then each beneficiary can decide whether or not to accelerate his/her respective rights to the future installments from time to time. In essence, one beneficiary can accelerate distributions if the need arises, while the other beneficiary may take the required minimum distributions. Obviously, more effective tax planning can then be done for each beneficiary if they are treated separately. A beneficiary may be in a low income tax bracket and may decide to accelerate distributions in order to increase current cash flow. Another beneficiary may be in a high income tax bracket and decide to take only the required minimum distribution in order to save on income taxes.

Direct Transfer Option for IRA Beneficiary:

The following questions and answers illustrate the distribution options of an IRA beneficiary following the death of the account owner before the required beginning date, with a special focus on the direct transfer rules.

Question 8.51: *Dr. Jerome Bordon is age 65 in 1995. He has selected his daughter, Joyce, who is age 42 in 1995, as the designated beneficiary of his IRA with the XYZ mutual fund. The IRA currently has a value of approximately $100,000. If Dr. Bordon dies on June 1, 1997, what distribution options are available for Joyce?*

Answer: Because Dr. Bordon died at age 67 prior to his required beginning date, the terms of his IRA plan document may permit Joyce to choose between the five-year rule or the life expectancy exception to the five-year rule. Dr. Bordon's required beginning date would have been April 1 of the calendar year following his attainment of age 70^1/$_2$.

Question 8.52: *May Joyce be required to use the five-year rule?*

Answer: Perhaps. If the IRA document mandates the five-year rule, then Joyce may not elect out of the five-year rule. If the IRA document permits Joyce to elect out of the five-year rule, then she must make a timely written election to follow the life expectancy distribution rules. If she fails to act timely, then she will default into the five-year rule. Under the five-year rule, Joyce would have to receive the entire balance of the IRA account no later than December 31, 2002. This deadline is the end of the fifth year following the year of Dr. Bordon's death (1997).

Question 8.53: *If the terms of Dr. Bordon's plan permit Joyce as the designated beneficiary to avoid the five-year distribution rule, how does she make the election?*

Answer: To elect out of the five-year rule, Joyce should send the IRA institution a written election by no later than December 31, 1998 (the end of the year following the year of her father's death). The form of the written election was previously discussed in this chapter. This is also the deadline for Joyce to begin the required minimum distributions from the IRA. In the written election, Joyce should state that she wishes to receive her required minimum distributions from her father's IRA over her 37.7-year life expectancy. On her birthday in the calendar year 1998, she attains age 45 and under the IRS single life expectancy table shown in the Appendix of this book, the life expectancy of a 45-year-old is 37.7 years.

Question 8.54: *Upon Dr. Bordon's death, may Joyce roll over Dr. Bordon's account into her own IRA?*

Answer: No. Joyce may not roll over her father's IRA. In the case of individuals dying after December 31, 1983, the surviving spouse is the only designated beneficiary who may roll over the IRA death benefits into his or her own IRA.

Question 8.55: *What would happen if Joyce in 1998 rolled over Dr. Bordon's IRA into her own IRA?*

Answer: The IRS would tax Joyce on the entire proceeds of Dr. Bordon's IRA, since the rollover was improper. In addition, the IRS will assess civil penalties against Joyce as well.

Question 8.56: *Upon Dr. Bordon's death, should the IRA account be maintained in Dr. Bordon's name?*

Answer: Yes. In order for the tax-deferred growth of the IRA to continue after Dr. Bordon's death, the IRA must be maintained in his name.

Question 8.57: *What approach should be used in order to maintain the tax-deferred growth of Dr. Bordon's IRA after his death?*

Answer: The account title of the IRA should be changed to read Jerome Bordon, deceased, Individual Retirement Account (date of death, June 1, 1997) for the benefit of Joyce Bordon, designated beneficiary. The IRA account should use the social security number of Joyce Bordon after Jerome Bordon's death. The account title could be shortened to read, "Jerome Bordon, deceased, IRA (DOD June 1, 1997), FBO Joyce Bordon, SS #100-00-0000."

Question 8.58: *If Joyce would like to transfer the IRA account maintained in the decedent's name to another IRA institution, may she do so?*

Answer: Yes. The IRS has taken a practical approach and permits a direct transfer to be made from one IRA institution to another as long as the IRA is maintained in the name of the deceased IRA owner.

For example, Joyce may direct that the assets be transferred from IRA No.1 to IRA No.2. The IRS allows the direct transfer and permits the tax deferred status of the IRA to be continued as long as the IRA is maintained in the name of the deceased IRA owner. Joyce, as the designated beneficiary, controls the IRA account under state law and can control the investments that are made in the decedent's IRA.

Question 8.59: *Must Joyce pay income taxes on the direct transfer of assets from the Jerome Bordon, deceased IRA No. 1 to the Jerome Bordon, deceased IRA No. 2?*

Answer: No. The direct transfer of assets from one IRA custodian to another IRA custodian does not result in a taxable event to Joyce as long as the IRA account is maintained in the decedent's name.

Question 8.60: *Is Joyce considered to have rolled over the decedent's IRA assets when the assets are transferred from IRA No. 1 to IRA No. 2 as described in the previous question?*

Answer: No. The IRS does not consider the transfer of IRA assets directly from IRA No. 1 to IRA No. 2 to be a rollover transaction. For the transfer to be considered a direct transfer and not a rollover, the transfer of funds must be directly from one IRA custodian to another IRA custodian. Joyce should not receive a check payable to her from IRA No.1 and then transfer it to IRA No.2. That would be an improper rollover transaction.

Question 8.61: *Could Joyce transfer a portion of IRA No. 1 to IRA No. 2 and a portion to IRA No. 3?*

Answer: Yes. The IRS has taken a liberal point of view and it places no limitations on the number of IRAs that can be maintained for the decreased IRA owner.

Question 8.62: *Is there a limitation on the number of IRA transfers that Joyce can make with respect to the decedent's IRA in a given period?*

Answer: No. There is no limitation on the number of direct IRA transfers that Joyce can make in a given period with respect to the decedent's IRA.

Question 8.63: *If Joyce divides her father's IRA into IRA No. 1, IRA No. 2 and IRA No. 3, must she receive her required minimum distributions from each IRA on a proportionate basis?*

Answer: No. The IRS has taken a practical approach and permits the required minimum distributions that Joyce must receive for a given calendar year to be taken from one or more of the IRAs. Thus, if the total of the required minimum distributions from all three IRAs is $3,500 for the calendar year 2001, Joyce may receive distributions from any one of the IRAs, or any combination of the IRAs as she prefers, as long as at least $3,500 is received in the year 2001.

Question 8.64: *If Joyce wishes to make a direct transfer of her father's IRA to another IRA institution, what should she first look into?*

Answer: Joyce should make certain that the other IRA institution permits the exception to the five-year rule to be operative. She should not transfer the decedent's IRA assets to an IRA institution that only has a five-year rule. In addition, if the exception to the five-year rule is permissible, she should file a copy of the timely written election that she previously made with the initial IRA custodian with the new institution. In fact, she should always check the IRA institution's plan document before she directs a transfer to that IRA institution. She should speak with a responsible official at the new institution before the transfer to make sure that the new institution will make payments to her based upon the life expectancy exception to the five-year rule. In addition, she should make sure that the new institution opens the new IRA in the name of the decedent.

Question 8.65: *Are the same IRS distribution rules applicable to IRA institutions that are called trustees instead of custodians?*

Answer: Yes. Direct transfers from an IRA custodian or an IRA trustee to an IRA custodian or an IRA trustee are nontaxable transfers. Thus, a direct transfer from an IRA custodian to an IRA trustee is a nontaxable transaction.

Question 8.66: *What should Joyce do in order to make sure that direct transfers of the decedent's IRAs are handled properly?*

Answer: Joyce should give written instructions to the decedent's IRA institution that the IRA assets should be directly transferred to the receiving IRA institution. The appropriate application should be completed for the receiving IRA institution indicating that the IRA account is in the decedent's name.

Joyce should speak to the transferring IRA institution to make sure that the institution does not make the check out to Joyce. If the transferring IRA institution does in fact make out the check to Joyce, it should not be negotiated but rather returned to the transferring IRA institution immediately. The check should be voided.

In addition, Joyce should advise the receiving IRA institution that under no circumstances should the decedent's IRA be titled in Joyce's name as an IRA owner. It is best to speak to a responsible official in each institution's IRA retirement department who is familiar with these rules and to follow up the point in writing with the responsible official in each IRA institution. It is imperative that the IRA account be maintained in the decedent's name in order to avoid an immediate taxable event to Joyce. An error in handling this issue can wipe out decades of tax-deferred growth. Joyce should not deal with clerical staff who are not familiar with these important issues.

Question 8.67: *Is there anything else Joyce should do in planning a direct transfer?*

Answer: Joyce should make sure that the new IRA institution is willing to pay out the decedent's IRA distributions under the life expectancy method. On occasion, a financial institution maintaining an IRA has indicated a preference towards not paying out the decedent's IRA death benefits over an extended period of time even though an election under the life expectancy method was made. If that is the case, then the designated beneficiary should immediately arrange for a direct transfer of the decedent's IRA assets to another IRA institution.

Multiple IRA Beneficiaries:

Special considerations may apply if you are planning to name more than one beneficiary for your IRA, as discussed in the following questions and answers.

Question 8.68: *Stuart Felding has his 67th birthday on May 12, 1995. He has a rollover IRA account that at the end of 1995 has a balance of approximately $700,000 with the XYZ brokerage firm. His wife, Janice, is age 65 in 1995 and their only child, Gary, is age 42 in 1995. Stuart has designated both his wife and his son as the designated beneficiaries of his IRA account. Each designated beneficiary has a 50% interest in Stuart's IRA account with the XYZ brokerage firm. If Stuart dies in 1996 at age 68, when must Gary commence his required minimum distributions from Stuart's IRA account?*

Answer: Stuart died before his required beginning date (April 1 of the year following the year he would have reached age 70$^{1}/_{2}$). Assume the terms of Stuart's IRA permit Gary to elect the life expectancy rule instead of the five-year rule. If Gary wants to make the life expectancy election, then he must make the election in writing and commence his required minimum distributions from his 50% interest in his father's IRA account by no later than December 31, 1997. This deadline is the end of the year following the year of Stuart's death (1996).

If the terms of Stuart's IRA made the five-year rule mandatory, or if the five-year rule applied as the IRA's default option upon Gary's failure to timely elect the life expectancy rule, then Gary would be required to receive his entire 50% share of Stuart's IRA by December 31, 2001, the end of the fifth year following Stuart's death.

Question 8.69: *Under the facts of Question 8.68, what options are available to Janice?*

Answer: Janice may use the designated beneficiary rule or the spousal IRA rollover rules. These rules were previously discussed in detail in Chapter 3.

Question 8.70: *Assuming Gary elects the life expectancy rule, what is Gary's life expectancy for purposes of calculating his required minimum distributions from Stuart's IRA?*

Answer: Gary is deemed to be his mother's age. Under the IRS rules, if more than one individual is selected as a designated beneficiary, then the designated beneficiary with the shortest life expectancy is used in order to determine the period over which the required minimum distributions must be made. Gary must, therefore, use Janice's life expectancy as determined in 1997. At age 67 in 1997, Janice's life expectancy is 18.4 years, as shown in the IRS single life expectancy table in the Appendix. Gary must, therefore, make the appropriate timely written election with the IRA institution to receive his required minimum distributions based upon a life expectancy of 18.4 years. Again, this assumes that the IRA plan document permits election of the life expectancy rule and does not mandate the five-year rule.

Question 8.71: *Is there an exception to the rule described above about Gary being deemed to be Janice's age?*

Answer: Yes. The IRS has a narrow exception for instances in which the IRA account is divided into separate accounts for the benefit of each designated beneficiary. Unfortunately, the IRS as of this date has not issued any letter rulings on what constitutes a separate account. In the absence of a letter ruling, one cannot take the chance that the separate account exception is available in the situation where Stuart has named Janice and Gary equally as the designated beneficiaries of his IRA account.

Question 8.72: *Is there anything that Stuart could do prior to his death that would permit Gary to use his own life expectancy for purposes of calculating his required minimum distributions after Stuart's death?*

Answer: Yes. Stuart should establish two IRA accounts with each account having approximately $350,000 in it. He should name Janice as the designated beneficiary of IRA No. 1 and Gary as the designated beneficiary of IRA No. 2. In this instance Gary can use his life expectancy instead of Janice's life expectancy in calculating his required minimum distributions for the calendar year 1997. In 1997 Gary is age 44 and his life expectancy is 38.7 years under the IRS table shown in the Appendix. Simply by opening up two IRAs instead of one IRA, Stuart has greatly enhanced the period over which Gary may receive his required minimum distributions from 18.4 years (based upon Janice's life expectancy) to 38.7 years (based upon Gary's life expectancy). Gary would make the appropriate timely written election with the IRA institution based upon his life expectancy of 38.7 years.

Question 8.73: *Assume that at Stuart's death in 1996 the IRA account at XYZ brokerage firm is valued at $750,000. Stuart had named his wife, Janice, and his son, Gary, as his designated beneficiaries as previously described in Question 8.68. As before, each designated beneficiary has a 50% interest in the IRA account. Gary is deemed to be his mother's age and must therefore use her life expectancy of 18 (18.4 years rounded down to 18 years for illustrative purposes) years in order to determine his required minimum distributions. Assume that the required minimum distributions are based upon a 7% rate of return. How much money will Gary receive over the 18-year period based upon the required minimum distribution rules?*

Answer: Gary will receive total required minimum distributions over the 18-year period of $775,176.43. The following schedule illustrates the computation of the required minimum distributions over an 18-year period.

Initial amount: $375,000.00 (50% of $750,000), Earnings: 7%

Distributions over 18 years

Year	Earnings at 7%	Required Minimum Distribution	Balance
			$375,000.00
1	$26,250.00	$20,833.33	380,416.67
2	26,629.17	22,377.45	384,668.39
3	26,926.79	24,041.77	387,553.41
4	27,128.74	25,836.89	388,845.26
5	27,219.17	27,774.66	388,289.77
6	27,180.28	29,868.44	385,601.61
7	26,992.11	32,133.47	380,460.25
8	26,632.22	34,587.30	372,505.17
9	26,075.36	37,250.52	361,330.01
10	25,293.10	40,147.78	346,475.33

cont'd

(continued from previous page)

Year	Earnings at 7%	Required Minimum Distribution	Balance
11	24,253.27	43,309.42	327,419.18
12	22,919.34	46,774.17	303,564.35
13	21,249.50	50,594.06	274,219.79
14	19,195.39	54,843.96	238,571.22
15	16,699.99	59,642.81	195,628.40
16	13,693.99	65,209.47	144,112.92
17	10,087.90	72,056.46	82,144.36
18	5,750.11	87,894.47	0.00
	$400,176.43	$775,176.43	

Question 8.74: *Assume that as in the answer to Question 8.72, Stuart has established two separate IRA accounts. Janice is the designated beneficiary of IRA No. 1 and Gary is the designated beneficiary of IRA No. 2. At Stuart's death in 1996, IRA No. 2 is valued at $375,000. In this instance, Gary, as the designated beneficiary of the separate IRA account, can use his life expectancy in calculating his required minimum distributions. Gary's life expectancy is 38 (38.7 years rounded down to 38 years for illustrative purposes) years in order to determine his required minimum distributions. Assume that the required minimum distributions are based upon a 7% rate of return. How much money will Gary receive over the 38-year period based upon the required minimum distribution rules?*

Answer: Gary will receive total required minimum distributions over the 38-year period of $1,908,632.38. The following schedule illustrates the computation of the required minimum distributions over a 38-year period.

Initial amount: $375,000.00, Earnings: 7%

Distributions over 38 years

Year	Earnings at 7%	Required Minimum Distribution	Balance
			375,000.00
1	$26,250.00	$9,868.42	391,381.58
2	27,396.71	10,577.88	408,200.41
3	28,574.03	11,338.90	425,435.54
4	29,780.49	12,155.30	443,060.73
5	31,014.25	13,031.20	461,043.78
6	32,273.06	13,971.02	479,345.82
7	33,554.21	14,979.56	497,920.47
8	34,854.43	16,061.95	516,712.95
9	36,169.91	17,223.77	535,659.09
10	37,496.14	18,471.00	554,684.23

(continued from previous page)

Year	Earnings at 7%	Required Minimum Distribution	Balance
11	38,827.90	19,810.15	573,701.98
12	40,159.14	21,248.22	592,612.90
13	41,482.90	22,792.80	611,303.00
14	42,791.21	24,452.12	629,642.09
15	44,074.95	26,235.09	647,481.95
16	45,323.74	28,151.39	664,654.30
17	46,525.80	30,211.56	680,968.54
18	47,667.80	32,427.07	696,209.27
19	48,734.65	34,810.46	710,133.46
20	49,709.34	37,375.45	722,467.35
21	50,572.71	40,137.08	732,902.98
22	51,303.21	43,111.94	741,094.25
23	51,876.60	46,318.39	746,652.46
24	52,265.67	49,776.83	749,141.30
25	52,439.89	53,510.09	748,071.10
26	52,364.98	57,543.93	742,892.15
27	52,002.45	61,907.68	732,986.92
28	51,309.08	66,635.17	717,660.83
29	50,236.26	71,766.08	696,131.01
30	48,729.17	77,347.89	667,512.29
31	46,725.86	83,439.04	630,799.11
32	44,155.94	90,114.16	584,840.89
33	40,938.86	97,473.48	528,306.27
34	36,981.44	105,661.25	459,626.46
35	32,173.85	114,906.62	376,893.69
36	26,382.56	125,631.23	277,645.02
37	19,435.15	138,822.51	158,257.66
38	11,078.04	169,335.70	0.00
	$1,533,632.38	$1,908,632.38	

Question 8.75: *Assume that Stuart has selected his estate as a beneficiary of 50% of his IRA and Gary as a designated beneficiary for the other 50% of his IRA. Stuart dies in 1996 at age 68. May Gary elect out of the five-year rule?*

Answer: No. When an IRA owner dies before his required beginning date, the IRS rules say that if an entity, as opposed to an individual, has been named as a beneficiary, then the IRA owner will be treated as having no designated beneficiary. If an estate is named as a beneficiary and the IRA owner dies before his required beginning date, the estate is treated as having no life expectancy. Under the IRS rules it is irrelevant that individuals have been designated as beneficiaries in addition to the estate. Under this scenario,

Gary may not elect out of the five-year rule. If the stakes are high enough, Gary should try to obtain a letter ruling from the IRS arguing that the separate account rule (Question 8.71) is applicable and that the five-year rule for Gary is not automatic.

Question 8.76: *What should Stuart do if he wishes his estate to receive 50% of his IRA upon his death and Gary to receive the other 50%?*

Answer: As previously described, Stuart should establish two IRAs. IRA No. 1 should be payable to his estate and IRA No. 2 should be payable to Gary. In that way Gary can definitely elect out of the five-year rule if Stuart dies before his required beginning date. This would enable Gary to receive required minimum distributions from IRA No. 2 over his life expectancy.

Making a Protective Election of the Life Expectancy Method for Your Beneficiary:

In certain cases, an IRA owner may want to specify the life expectancy distribution method for his or her beneficiary, as discussed in the following questions and answers.

Question 8.77: *Judy Clark, an IRA owner, would like to know if she can make an election as to the distribution method that would apply to her designated beneficiary if she dies prior to her required beginning date. May an IRA owner elect the distribution method on behalf of his or her designated beneficiary, or must the election decision be left to the designated beneficiary?*

Answer: The IRA document may permit the IRA owner to make an election. An IRA document may permit either the IRA owner or the designated beneficiary to elect whether the five-year rule or the life expectancy exception to the five-year rule will apply in instances where the IRA owner dies prior to his required beginning date.

Question 8.78: *Why would an IRA owner want to make the election as to which distribution method should be used by his or her designated beneficiary?*

Answer: An IRA owner may wish to make a protective election if, for example, he or she is seriously ill and does not expect to live until the required beginning date. An IRA owner may also wish to make the election on behalf of an adult designated beneficiary if the designated beneficiary is unsophisticated in tax matters.

Keep in mind that even if the IRA owner wishes to make a protective election, the election may not be permitted under the terms of the IRA document.

Question 8.79: *If the designated beneficiary is not sophisticated in tax matters, and the terms of the IRA document permit the IRA owner to make the election, then what type of election is recommended?*

Answer: It is probably best to elect the life expectancy exception to the five-year rule, thereby allowing distributions to be spread over a longer period of time.

Question 8.80: *Assume that Judy Clark is the IRA owner and her adult nephew, Philip Clark, is her designated beneficiary. Further assume that Judy's required beginning date is April 1, 1997. Philip is not sophisticated in tax matters and Judy wishes to make a protective election of the life expectancy distribution method. Assuming that the terms of her IRA document allow Judy to do so, how should she make this election?*

Answer: The IRA institution may not have a specific form for the election. In that case, Judy, as the IRA owner, would have to create her own election form. The form should be served, together with a covering letter by certified mail, return receipt requested, upon the IRA institution. The election should refer to the IRA account number and should state the following:

> In the event that I, Judy Clark, should die before my required beginning date of April 1, 1997, and if my designated beneficiary of this IRA account #1001 at the date of my death is my nephew, Philip Clark, and if he survives me, then the required minimum distributions of this IRA account #1001 with your institution shall be paid to Philip Clark over a period not to exceed the life expectancy of Philip Clark based upon his life expectancy under the IRS life expectancy tables as determined in the calendar year following the year after my date of death. Distributions shall not be paid to Philip Clark under the five-year rule. In addition, Philip Clark may accelerate distributions from this IRA account at any time and from time to time. This IRA account title shall remain titled in my name after my death and during the entire distribution period that payments are made to Philip Clark.
>
> Furthermore, this IRA account may be directly transferred fully or partially to any other IRA institution after my death by my nephew, Philip Clark, if he is the designated beneficiary of this IRA at the date of my death and provided that the IRA account is still maintained and titled in my name. This election as to the life expectancy method shall still be applicable after any such transfer to any transferee IRA.

The election must be signed and dated by Judy Clark, the IRA owner. Additional copies of the election should be made and given to Philip Clark so that if the IRA account is transferred to another IRA institution by Philip after Judy's death there is additional evidence of the fact that the life expectancy rule rather than the five-year rule applies.

This sample election is illustrative only. The actual written election should be prepared in conjunction with your professional advisor or estate planner and must be based upon the laws and rules in effect at the time the election is made. The election should be revised from time to time to reflect any changes in the law and in the IRS rules.

Question 8.81: *What is the advantage of having Judy make the election out of the five-year rule on behalf of her nephew, Philip?*

Answer: If Philip is not sophisticated in tax matters then Judy's election will prevent him from defaulting into the five-year rule should Judy die before her required beginning date. In essence, Judy has given Philip a road map to guide him through the complex maze of IRS rules. Judy's election out of the five-year rule has given Philip an extended payout period while also allowing him the greatest degree of flexibility since he can always accelerate the required minimum distributions from time to time. The only disadvantage in this approach is that under the life expectancy rule, required minimum distributions must commence to Philip by December 31 of the calendar year following Judy's year of death. Again, the election out of the five-year rule will only be required if Judy dies before her required beginning date.

Question 8.82: *Is there any other situation where the IRA owner would make a protective written election as to the method of payment?*

Answer: Yes. If there is a concern that the IRA owner will not live until his or her required beginning date and the designated beneficiary is a minor, then a protective election should be made.

Question 8.83: *Why should the IRA owner bother making a protective written election as to a method of payment of the IRA death benefits in the event a minor is involved?*

Answer: Based upon state law, a minor may not legally have the capacity to designate a method of payment. Therefore, the minor would probably default into the five-year rule if the IRA owner should die before his or her required beginning date. Most IRA documents provide that the default option is the five-year rule when the designated beneficiary is other than the spouse. In order to avoid this problem, and to provide an extended payout period for the minor, the IRA owner should select a method of payment based upon the minor's life expectancy that will come into play if the IRA owner should die before his or her required beginning date.

Question 8.84: *Assume that the designated beneficiary is a minor who may not legally elect a method of payment. What happens if the IRA document does not permit the IRA owner, prior to his or her death, to make a protective election as to a method of payment?*

Answer: If the IRA owner dies before his or her required beginning date and the distributions are payable to a minor, then the default option is generally the five-year rule.

To avoid this default option, an IRA owner who has named a minor as a designated beneficiary should only use an IRA institution that has an IRA document that permits a protective election of the life expectancy rule in the event that the IRA owner dies before his or her required beginning date.

Question 8.85: *Why can't the minor's parent make the election out of the five-year rule?*

Answer: The parent, as the natural guardian of the minor, generally has no power under state law to make an election on behalf of the minor as to the method of payment of IRA distributions.

Question 8.86: *Instead of directly naming a minor as the designated beneficiary of the IRA, would it be better to select a Custodian or an irrevocable trust to receive the IRA assets on the minor's behalf?*

Answer: Yes. As discussed in Chapter 5, there are advantages in naming a Custodian or an irrevocable trust to receive the IRA assets on the minor's behalf upon the IRA owner's death.

CHAPTER 9

Estate Planning with Retirement Assets

Many taxpayers accumulate substantial assets in qualified plans, 403(b) annuity contracts, and Individual Retirement Accounts (IRAs). During their lifetimes these arrangements provide the vehicle for many taxpayers to live without the pressure of the need to accumulate additional wealth for retirement. However, as the aging of taxpayers in the United States takes place, many people find that their retirement plan assets have accumulated to a point that the family is exposed to substantial tax liabilities.

Taxpayers who have accumulated substantial retirement assets must recognize that they must deal with an estate tax liability problem. They must also understand that these retirement assets are subject to income taxes and, in some instances, subject to an excess accumulation tax in your estate. Improper planning and poor advice may wipe out most of the retirement assets. The estate tax liability for purposes of this chapter is limited to the federal estate tax liability and does not consider state estate tax liabilities or any potential excess accumulation tax liability.

Depending on the amount of your total assets from retirement plans and other holdings, estate planning can be an involved process, requiring the expertise of an experienced tax practitioner. This chapter is designed only as an introduction to the issues which you and your advisor will face in salvaging your retirement assets for the benefit of your family.

Question 9.1: *What type of advisor should you engage in order to do effective estate planning with your retirement assets?*

Answer: The advisor that you select must be knowledgeable in estate planning. In addition, he or she must be familiar with the retirement plan distribution rules and be able to integrate the retirement plan with the estate plan.

Ask the advisor for references and ask if he or she has had prior experience involving tax planning for clients with substantial retirement accounts.

Question 9.2: *Why is it difficult to find an advisor who can integrate the estate plan with the retirement plan?*

Answer: The advisor must have a broad base of knowledge in many areas, such as the following:

a. Knowledge of income taxation of estates and trusts.

b. Knowledge of estate taxation (federal and state).

c. Knowledge of state law apportionment statutes.

d. Knowledge of state estate tax and/or state inheritance laws.

e. Knowledge of property law concepts.

f. Knowledge of pension distribution rules.

g. Knowledge of pension excise tax rules, i.e., penalties.

h. Knowledge of the probate laws of the state.

Question 9.3: *If your advisor lacks expertise in all of these areas, what should you do?*

Answer: Ask your advisor to help you retain a knowledgeable specialist to provide assistance in developing a comprehensive estate plan that integrates your retirement assets with your overall estate plan.

Question 9.4: *Why is there such a concern about integrating your retirement assets with your estate plan?*

Answer: Retirement assets pose a special tax problem since these retirement assets may be subject to a triple tax. Retirement assets may be subject to estate tax, income tax, and pension excise taxes (penalties).

Question 9.5: *If all the retirement assets are payable to my surviving spouse, then aren't my estate tax problems eliminated?*

Answer: Maybe. If when your spouse dies, his or her taxable estate is less than $600,000, then the federal estate tax problem is eliminated under current law. However, if your spouse predeceases you and you have more than $600,000 in your taxable estate, then there is a federal estate tax liability upon your death.

Congress may increase the estate tax threshold above $600,000. When this book went to press, Congress was considering legislation that would raise the threshold to $700,000 for estates of persons dying in 1996, $725,000 in 1997 and $750,000 in 1998, with subsequent annual increases for inflation.

Question 9.6: *If the taxable estate of each spouse is $600,000 or less, is the federal estate tax liability eliminated?*

Answer: Maybe. Generally, the federal estate tax liability would be eliminated in its entirety. There are certain technical exceptions to this general rule. If you made gifts in the past above certain limits, these gifts may trigger an estate tax even if your taxable estate is $600,000 or less. In addition, state estate tax or inheritance tax laws may be applicable. As noted in the answer to Question 9.5, the $600,000 estate tax floor may be raised by Congress.

Question 9.7: *Why should I be concerned about estate planning if all my assets are paid to my spouse upon my death?*

Answer: If you leave all your assets to your surviving spouse, then an estate tax liability may be triggered upon his or her subsequent death. There will be an estate tax liability on the subsequent death of your spouse if your spouse's taxable estate exceeds the estate tax floor, currently $600,000.

Illustrative Case:

The following questions and answers illustrate some planning options for a family where a retirement plan account is the largest asset.

Question 9.8: *I am a married college professor and have two children and two grandchildren. During my teaching career I have accumulated $650,000 in my 403(b) annuity contract. In addition, I have $200,000 in life insurance which I own. My wife is the beneficiary of my 403(b) annuity contract and of my life insurance. My spouse and I jointly own a residence (tenancy by entirety) which has (net of mortgage) a value of $250,000. I have $65,000 in a joint savings account and $60,000 in mutual funds that are jointly owned with my wife. Assume that I die first and my wife dies shortly thereafter. Is there an estate tax liability upon my death or upon the subsequent death of my spouse?*

Answer: While there is no federal estate tax liability on your death, there will be a federal estate tax liability upon the subsequent death of your spouse. The assets that are paid directly to your spouse upon your death qualify for the unlimited marital deduction. Therefore, there is no federal estate tax liability when you die. Upon the subsequent death of your spouse, the federal estate tax liability is approximately $235,000. This liability assumes the current law unified estate credit of $192,800 (which offsets $600,000 of estate tax liability) is applicable. The liability is computed as follows:

Retirement assets	$ 650,000
Life insurance proceeds	200,000
Residence	250,000
Savings account	65,000
Mutual funds	60,000
Gross estate	$ 1,225,000
Less: Expenses of administration (estimated)	25,000
Taxable estate	$ 1,200,000
Federal estate tax before credit	$ 427,800
Less: Federal unified credit	192,800
Federal estate tax	$ 235,000

Expenses of administration in the first estate are ignored and state estate taxes are not considered in the above example.

Question 9.9: *Is there anything that I can do before my death in order to eliminate the $235,000 federal estate tax liability described in Question 9.8 above?*

Answer: Yes. There are several ways to eliminate the federal estate tax liability of $235,000. One approach is to have the life insurance proceeds payable directly to your children and to transfer the 403(b) annuity contract proceeds into two brand new IRAs if the annuity contract has a cashout provision. One IRA could be in the amount of $410,000 and could be payable to your children, and the other IRA in the amount of $240,000 could be payable to your spouse. If the annuity contract does not have a cash out provision, then the designated beneficiaries of the annuity contract must be split in order to accomplish the result that is desired. The split approach is complex and a professional advisor must be consulted. The split designated beneficiary approach is not as desirable as the IRA approach under distribution payout rules. Under the split designated beneficiary approach, the children are generally deemed to be the age of the mother. Upon the subsequent death of your spouse, her federal estate tax liability will be approximately zero. This is computed as follows:

Retirement assets	$ 240,000
Life insurance proceeds	-0-
Residence	250,000
Savings account	65,000
Mutual funds	60,000
Gross estate	$ 615,000
Less: Expenses of administration (estimated)	15,000
Taxable estate	$ 600,000
Federal estate tax before credit	192,800
Less: Federal unified credit	192,800
Federal estate tax	$ -0-

Question 9.10: *Could the result in Question 9.9 be accomplished by shifting other items in the estate?*

Answer: Yes. Other assets could be partially used to accomplish the same result.

Question 9.11: *I thought that I could just change my will in order to avoid the estate tax liability described in Question 9.8. Doesn't that approach accomplish the same result?*

Answer: No. A will only operates on probate assets. A will does not govern what happens to nonprobate assets. The 403(b) annuity contract payable to an individual as a beneficiary, the life insurance policy payable to an individual as a beneficiary, the jointly held assets, and the real estate held as tenancy by the entirety are not controlled by the will since they are not considered to be probate assets.

Question 9.12: *What is a probate asset?*

Answer: A probate asset is an asset that is solely owned by the decedent or the proceeds of any non-probate asset such as a life insurance policy that is payable to the estate. The executor can only control those assets that come into his possession as probate assets.

Question 9.13: *My wife is unhappy about the suggestions to leave the life insurance and most of the retirement assets to our children because she feels that she will not have sufficient income to live comfortably in her retirement years. Is there any other approach that will give her more financial security and still save the children a substantial amount of federal estate tax?*

Answer: Yes. The beneficiary of the life insurance proceeds can be a trust (either revocable or irrevocable). The trust provisions could state that the trust income shall be paid to your surviving spouse during her lifetime. This would mean that your spouse receives an annual income from the trust. In addition, she may be given a 5% right of invasion of principal each year or $5,000, whichever is greater. The spouse should not generally be the trustee, because if she is given certain powers, it may result in the inclusion of the value of the life insurance proceeds in her estate for estate tax purposes. The children should be the trustees and should have the right in their absolute discretion to invade principal on behalf of their mother. If your spouse is a co-trustee, her powers should be limited to investment decisions and she should not have any discretionary powers over trust principal or any other discretionary powers except for investment decisions.

Question 9.14: *My wife still feels nervous and would like some additional security. Is there anything else that you can suggest to alleviate her anxiety?*

Answer: Yes. Assume that the annuity contract has a cashout provision. Upon your death as the IRA owner, the children will commence to take distributions from their inherited IRA. They may then lend the net proceeds after taxes to their mother. The loan should be evidenced by a long-term note and bear interest at the appropriate rate. The interest income and IRA payments will, of course, result in taxable income to the children but the estate tax savings will be well in excess of the increase in the income tax liability of the children. If the annuity contract does not have a cash out provision, the annuity contract beneficiary designations must be split between the spouse and the children. The children may then use the same loan approach as described for IRAs.

Question 9.15: *These steps seem to alleviate my estate tax problem if I die first. Would there be an estate tax problem if my wife died first?*

Answer: Yes. Although there would be no federal estate tax liability if your wife died first, upon your subsequent death shortly after your wife, your estate would be subject to the same federal estate tax liability of $235,000, see the answer to Question 9.8.

Question 9.16: *My wife and I would like you to recommend an approach to minimize the estate tax liability if my wife is ill and it looks as though she will predecease me. Assume that I survive my wife and die shortly thereafter. Do you have any suggestions?*

Answer: The jointly held residence (tenancy by entirety) with a net value of $250,000 should be deeded into your wife's name. The joint savings account of $65,000 should be retitled in your wife's name, as well as the mutual funds of $60,000. Your wife can then by will decide who should receive the residence, the savings account, and the mutual funds. Assume that she by will has these assets going to your children outright. On your subsequent death shortly thereafter your federal estate tax liability will be approximately $88,650. This liability is computed as follows:

Retirement assets	$ 650,000
Life insurance proceeds	200,000
Residence	-0-
Savings account	-0-
Mutual funds	-0-
Gross estate	$ 850,000
Less: Expenses of administration (estimated)	15,000
Taxable estate	$ 835,000
Federal estate tax before credit	$ 281,450
Less: Federal unified credit	192,800
Federal estate tax	$ 88,650

Question 9.17: *Assume that I am in good health. Can you suggest an approach to accomplish an even larger reduction in federal estate tax liability?*

Answer: An approach that most estate planners suggest is that the ownership of the life insurance policy be structured in a manner that avoids including the life insurance policy in the gross estate of either spouse. Most estate planners are familiar with the concept of the irrevocable life insurance trust and can structure a transfer of the life insurance policy to an irrevocable trust for the benefit of your wife or children. Alternatively, your children can be made the owners and beneficiaries of the life insurance policy.

If you transfer the ownership of the $200,000 life insurance policy to either an irrevocable life insurance trust or to your children and survive by more than three years, then the life insurance policy is not included in your gross estate. Thus, the federal estate tax liability of $88,650 would be reduced to approximately $12,950. This liability is computed as follows:

Retirement assets	$ 650,000
Life insurance proceeds	-0-
Residence	-0-
Savings account	-0-
Mutual funds	-0-
Gross estate	$ 650,000
Less: Expenses of administration (estimated)	15,000
Taxable estate	$ 635,000
Federal estate tax before credit	$ 205,750
Less: Federal unified credit	192,800
Federal estate tax	$ 12,950

Question 9.18: *I like your suggestion about transferring the life insurance policy out of my name. However, there is no guarantee that I will live for more than three years from the date of the transfer of the ownership of the life insurance policy to either an irrevocable trust or to my children. Is there anything else that I can do in order to reduce the $88,650 federal estate tax liability?*

Answer: You should consider making gifts to your children and to your grandchildren. Since you have two children and two grandchildren, you can make a $10,000 gift to each child and to each grandchild for a total of $40,000 of gifts in each calendar year. These gifts will not result in a reduction of your unified credit. In addition, your wife can agree to join in the gifts that you make, which will result in a doubling of the amount of gifts that you can make in each calendar year. Assume that you and your wife agree to maximize gifts over a two-year period since you are both in poor health. You and your wife can each make gifts of $40,000, or your wife can consent to your making gifts of $80,000 by filing the appropriate gift tax returns with the necessary consents.

It is best that the $80,000 of gifts be made from your assets. This is because you have $650,000 of retirement assets and because you will probably have to include the $200,000 of life insurance proceeds in your gross estate since you may not survive for the required three-year period after you transfer the ownership of your policy. You have only one asset that lends itself to a gift giving program. That asset unfortunately is a retirement asset that has never been taxed.

In order for you to net $80,000 each year (after federal and state income taxes) you will have to withdraw approximately $120,000 from your retirement assets on an annual basis. In two years you will withdraw $240,000 from your retirement assets. Assume you do this for a two-year period and then stop. Your children have assured you that if you need the money they will lend it to you. You agree that you will sign a note and pay a reasonable rate of interest on the note if you need to borrow the money from them at a later date. Assume that your wife predeceases you and you die shortly thereafter, but that two years of gifts have been consummated before your death. This can be accomplished since you can make the $80,000 worth of gifts in December of a calendar year and another $80,000 of gifts in January of the subsequent calendar year. Your wife consents to these gifts. Upon your death there is no federal estate tax liability. This zero liability is computed as follows:

Retirement assets ($650,000 less $240,000)	$ 410,000
Life insurance proceeds	200,000
Residence	-0-
Savings account	-0-
Mutual funds	-0-
Gross estate	$ 610,000
Less: Expenses of administration (estimated)	10,000
Taxable estate	$ 600,000
Federal estate tax before credit	$ 192,800
Less: Federal unified credit	192,800
Federal estate tax	$ -0-

The above illustration assumes that the earnings from the retirement assets have been applied towards living expenses.

Appendix

The following life expectancy tables are from IRS Publication 590, Appendix E. They reflect the tables in section 1.72–9 of the IRS regulations. Table I of Publication 590 reflects Table V of the regulations and Table II of Publication 590 reflects Table VI of the regulations.

The Table for Determining Applicable Divisor for MDIB (see Chapter 4 of this book) is also from Appendix E of the IRS Publication 590.

APPENDIX E. Table for Determining Applicable Divisor for MDIB (Minimum Distribution Incidental Benefit)

Age	Applicable divisor	Age	Applicable divisor
70	26.2	93	8.8
71	25.3	94	8.3
72	24.4	95	7.8
73	23.5	96	7.3
74	22.7	97	6.9
75	21.8	98	6.5
76	20.9	99	6.1
77	20.1	100	5.7
78	19.2	101	5.3
79	18.4	102	5.0
80	17.6	103	4.7
81	16.8	104	4.4
82	16.0	105	4.1
83	15.3	106	3.8
84	14.5	107	3.6
85	13.8	108	3.3
86	13.1	109	3.1
87	12.4	110	2.8
88	11.8	111	2.6
89	11.1	112	2.4
90	10.5	113	2.2
91	9.9	114	2.0
92	9.4	115 and older	1.8

APPENDIX E. Life Expectancy Tables

TABLE I			
(Single Life Expectancy)*			
AGE	DIVISOR	AGE	DIVISOR
35	47.3	73	13.9
36	46.4	74	13.2
37	45.4	75	12.5
38	44.4	76	11.9
39	43.5	77	11.2
40	42.5	78	10.6
41	41.5	79	10.0
42	40.6	80	9.5
43	39.6	81	8.9
44	38.7	82	8.4
45	37.7	83	7.9
46	36.8	84	7.4
47	35.9	85	6.9
48	34.9	86	6.5
49	34.0	87	6.1
50	33.1	88	5.7
51	32.2	89	5.3
52	31.3	90	5.0
53	30.4	91	4.7
54	29.5	92	4.4
55	28.6	93	4.1
56	27.7	94	3.9
57	26.8	95	3.7
58	25.9	96	3.4
59	25.0	97	3.2
60	24.2	98	3.0
61	23.3	99	2.8
62	22.5	100	2.7
63	21.6	101	2.5
64	20.8	102	2.3
65	20.0	103	2.1
66	19.2	104	1.9
67	18.4	105	1.8
68	17.6	106	1.6
69	16.8	107	1.4
70	16.0	108	1.3
71	15.3	109	1.1
72	14.6	110	1.0

* Table I does not provide for IRA owners younger than 35 years of age. For additional life expectancy tables, see Publication 939.

APPENDIX E. *(continued)*

TABLE II
(Joint Life and Last Survivor Expectancy)*

AGES	35	36	37	38	39	40	41	42	43	44
35	54.0	53.5	53.0	52.6	52.2	51.8	51.4	51.1	50.8	50.5
36	53.5	53.0	52.5	52.0	51.6	51.2	50.8	50.4	50.1	49.8
37	53.0	52.5	52.0	51.5	51.0	50.6	50.2	49.8	49.5	49.1
38	52.6	52.0	51.5	51.0	50.5	50.0	49.6	49.2	48.8	48.5
39	52.2	51.6	51.0	50.5	50.0	49.5	49.1	48.6	48.2	47.8
40	51.8	51.2	50.6	50.0	49.5	49.0	48.5	48.1	47.6	47.2
41	51.4	50.8	50.2	49.6	49.1	48.5	48.0	47.5	47.1	46.7
42	51.1	50.4	49.8	49.2	48.6	48.1	47.5	47.0	46.6	46.1
43	50.8	50.1	49.5	48.8	48.2	47.6	47.1	46.6	46.0	45.6
44	50.5	49.8	49.1	48.5	47.8	47.2	46.7	46.1	45.6	45.1
45	50.2	49.5	48.8	48.1	47.5	46.9	46.3	45.7	45.1	44.6
46	50.0	49.2	48.5	47.8	47.2	46.5	45.9	45.3	44.7	44.1
47	49.7	49.0	48.3	47.5	46.8	46.2	45.5	44.9	44.3	43.7
48	49.5	48.8	48.0	47.3	46.6	45.9	45.2	44.5	43.9	43.3
49	49.3	48.5	47.8	47.0	46.3	45.6	44.9	44.2	43.6	42.9
50	49.2	48.4	47.6	46.8	46.0	45.3	44.6	43.9	43.2	42.6
51	49.0	48.2	47.4	46.6	45.8	45.1	44.3	43.6	42.9	42.2
52	48.8	48.0	47.2	46.4	45.6	44.8	44.1	43.3	42.6	41.9
53	48.7	47.9	47.0	46.2	45.4	44.6	43.9	43.1	42.4	41.7
54	48.6	47.7	46.9	46.0	45.2	44.4	43.6	42.9	42.1	41.4
55	48.5	47.6	46.7	45.9	45.1	44.2	43.4	42.7	41.9	41.2
56	48.3	47.5	46.6	45.8	44.9	44.1	43.3	42.5	41.7	40.9
57	48.3	47.4	46.5	45.6	44.8	43.9	43.1	42.3	41.5	40.7
58	48.2	47.3	46.4	45.5	44.7	43.8	43.0	42.1	41.3	40.5
59	48.1	47.2	46.3	45.4	44.5	43.7	42.8	42.0	41.2	40.4
60	48.0	47.1	46.2	45.3	44.4	43.6	42.7	41.9	41.0	40.2
61	47.9	47.0	46.1	45.2	44.3	43.5	42.6	41.7	40.9	40.0
62	47.9	47.0	46.0	45.1	44.2	43.4	42.5	41.6	40.8	39.9
63	47.8	46.9	46.0	45.1	44.2	43.3	42.4	41.5	40.6	39.8
64	47.8	46.8	45.9	45.0	44.1	43.2	42.3	41.4	40.5	39.7
65	47.7	46.8	45.9	44.9	44.0	43.1	42.2	41.3	40.4	39.6
66	47.7	46.7	45.8	44.9	44.0	43.1	42.2	41.3	40.4	39.5
67	47.6	46.7	45.8	44.8	43.9	43.0	42.1	41.2	40.3	39.4
68	47.6	46.7	45.7	44.8	43.9	42.9	42.0	41.1	40.2	39.3
69	47.6	46.6	45.7	44.8	43.8	42.9	42.0	41.1	40.2	39.3
70	47.5	46.6	45.7	44.7	43.8	42.9	41.9	41.0	40.1	39.2
71	47.5	46.6	45.6	44.7	43.8	42.8	41.9	41.0	40.1	39.1
72	47.5	46.6	45.6	44.7	43.7	42.8	41.9	40.9	40.0	39.1
73	47.5	46.5	45.6	44.6	43.7	42.8	41.8	40.9	40.0	39.0
74	47.5	46.5	45.6	44.6	43.7	42.7	41.8	40.9	39.9	39.0
75	47.4	46.5	45.5	44.6	43.6	42.7	41.8	40.8	39.9	39.0
76	47.4	46.5	45.5	44.6	43.6	42.7	41.7	40.8	39.9	38.9
77	47.4	46.5	45.5	44.6	43.6	42.7	41.7	40.8	39.8	38.9
78	47.4	46.4	45.5	44.5	43.6	42.6	41.7	40.7	39.8	38.9
79	47.4	46.4	45.5	44.5	43.6	42.6	41.7	40.7	39.8	38.9
80	47.4	46.4	45.5	44.5	43.6	42.6	41.7	40.7	39.8	38.8
81	47.4	46.4	45.5	44.5	43.5	42.6	41.6	40.7	39.8	38.8
82	47.4	46.4	45.4	44.5	43.5	42.6	41.6	40.7	39.7	38.8
83	47.4	46.4	45.4	44.5	43.5	42.6	41.6	40.7	39.7	38.8
84	47.4	46.4	45.4	44.5	43.5	42.6	41.6	40.7	39.7	38.8
85	47.4	46.4	45.4	44.5	43.5	42.6	41.6	40.7	39.7	38.8
86	47.3	46.4	45.4	44.5	43.5	42.5	41.6	40.6	39.7	38.8
87	47.3	46.4	45.4	44.5	43.5	42.5	41.6	40.6	39.7	38.7
88	47.3	46.4	45.4	44.5	43.5	42.5	41.6	40.6	39.7	38.7
89	47.3	46.4	45.4	44.4	43.5	42.5	41.6	40.6	39.7	38.7
90	47.3	46.4	45.4	44.4	43.5	42.5	41.6	40.6	39.7	38.7
91	47.3	46.4	45.4	44.4	43.5	42.5	41.6	40.6	39.7	38.7
92	47.3	46.4	45.4	44.4	43.5	42.5	41.6	40.6	39.7	38.7

* Table II does not provide for IRA owners or survivors younger than 35 years of age. For additional life expectancy tables, see IRS Publication 939.

APPENDIX E. (continued)

TABLE II (continued)
(Joint Life and Last Survivor Expectancy)

AGES	45	46	47	48	49	50	51	52	53	54
45	44.1	43.6	43.2	42.7	42.3	42.0	41.6	41.3	41.0	40.7
46	43.6	43.1	42.6	42.2	41.8	41.4	41.0	40.6	40.3	40.0
47	43.2	42.6	42.1	41.7	41.2	40.8	40.4	40.0	39.7	39.3
48	42.7	42.2	41.7	41.2	40.7	40.2	39.8	39.4	39.0	38.7
49	42.3	41.8	41.2	40.7	40.2	39.7	39.3	38.8	38.4	38.1
50	42.0	41.4	40.8	40.2	39.7	39.2	38.7	38.3	37.9	37.5
51	41.6	41.0	40.4	39.8	39.3	38.7	38.2	37.8	37.3	36.9
52	41.3	40.6	40.0	39.4	38.8	38.3	37.8	37.3	36.8	36.4
53	41.0	40.3	39.7	39.0	38.4	37.9	37.3	36.8	36.3	35.8
54	40.7	40.0	39.3	38.7	38.1	37.5	36.9	36.4	35.8	35.3
55	40.4	39.7	39.0	38.4	37.7	37.1	36.5	35.9	35.4	34.9
56	40.2	39.5	38.7	38.1	37.4	36.8	36.1	35.6	35.0	34.4
57	40.0	39.2	38.5	37.8	37.1	36.4	35.8	35.2	34.6	34.0
58	39.7	39.0	38.2	37.5	36.8	36.1	35.5	34.8	34.2	33.6
59	39.6	38.8	38.0	37.3	36.6	35.9	35.2	34.5	33.9	33.3
60	39.4	38.6	37.8	37.1	36.3	35.6	34.9	34.2	33.6	32.9
61	39.2	38.4	37.6	36.9	36.1	35.4	34.6	33.9	33.3	32.6
62	39.1	38.3	37.5	36.7	35.9	35.1	34.4	33.7	33.0	32.3
63	38.9	38.1	37.3	36.5	35.7	34.9	34.2	33.5	32.7	32.0
64	38.8	38.0	37.2	36.3	35.5	34.8	34.0	33.2	32.5	31.8
65	38.7	37.9	37.0	36.2	35.4	34.6	33.8	33.0	32.3	31.6
66	38.6	37.8	36.9	36.1	35.2	34.4	33.6	32.9	32.1	31.4
67	38.5	37.7	36.8	36.0	35.1	34.3	33.5	32.7	31.9	31.2
68	38.4	37.6	36.7	35.8	35.0	34.2	33.4	32.5	31.8	31.0
69	38.4	37.5	36.6	35.7	34.9	34.1	33.2	32.4	31.6	30.8
70	38.3	37.4	36.5	35.7	34.8	34.0	33.1	32.3	31.5	30.7
71	38.2	37.3	36.5	35.6	34.7	33.9	33.0	32.2	31.4	30.5
72	38.2	37.3	36.4	35.5	34.6	33.8	32.9	32.1	31.2	30.4
73	38.1	37.2	36.3	35.4	34.6	33.7	32.8	32.0	31.1	30.3
74	38.1	37.2	36.3	35.4	34.5	33.6	32.8	31.9	31.1	30.2
75	38.1	37.1	36.2	35.3	34.5	33.6	32.7	31.8	31.0	30.1
76	38.0	37.1	36.2	35.3	34.4	33.5	32.6	31.8	30.9	30.1
77	38.0	37.1	36.2	35.3	34.4	33.5	32.6	31.7	30.8	30.0
78	38.0	37.0	36.1	35.2	34.3	33.4	32.5	31.7	30.8	29.9
79	37.9	37.0	36.1	35.2	34.3	33.4	32.5	31.6	30.7	29.9
80	37.9	37.0	36.1	35.2	34.2	33.4	32.5	31.6	30.7	29.8
81	37.9	37.0	36.0	35.1	34.2	33.3	32.4	31.5	30.7	29.8
82	37.9	36.9	36.0	35.1	34.2	33.3	32.4	31.5	30.6	29.7
83	37.9	36.9	36.0	35.1	34.2	33.3	32.4	31.5	30.6	29.7
84	37.8	36.9	36.0	35.1	34.2	33.2	32.3	31.4	30.6	29.7
85	37.8	36.9	36.0	35.1	34.1	33.2	32.3	31.4	30.5	29.6
86	37.8	36.9	36.0	35.0	34.1	33.2	32.3	31.4	30.5	29.6
87	37.8	36.9	35.9	35.0	34.1	33.2	32.3	31.4	30.5	29.6
88	37.8	36.9	35.9	35.0	34.1	33.2	32.3	31.4	30.5	29.6
89	37.8	36.9	35.9	35.0	34.1	33.2	32.3	31.4	30.5	29.6
90	37.8	36.9	35.9	35.0	34.1	33.2	32.3	31.3	30.5	29.6
91	37.8	36.8	35.9	35.0	34.1	33.2	32.2	31.3	30.4	29.5
92	37.8	36.8	35.9	35.0	34.1	33.2	32.2	31.3	30.4	29.5

APPENDIX E. Life Expectancy Tables (continued)

TABLE II (continued)
(Joint Life and Last Survivor Expectancy)

AGES	55	56	57	58	59	60	61	62	63	64	65	66	67	68	69	70	71	72	73	74
55	34.4	33.9	33.5	33.1	32.7	32.3	32.0	31.7	31.4	31.1										
56	33.9	33.4	33.0	32.5	32.1	31.7	31.4	31.0	30.7	30.4										
57	33.5	33.0	32.5	32.0	31.6	31.2	30.8	30.4	30.1	29.8										
58	33.1	32.5	32.0	31.5	31.1	30.6	30.2	29.9	29.5	29.2										
59	32.7	32.1	31.6	31.1	30.6	30.1	29.7	29.3	28.9	28.6										
60	32.3	31.7	31.2	30.6	30.1	29.7	29.2	28.8	28.4	28.0										
61	32.0	31.4	30.8	30.2	29.7	29.2	28.7	28.3	27.8	27.4										
62	31.7	31.0	30.4	29.9	29.3	28.8	28.3	27.8	27.3	26.9										
63	31.4	30.7	30.1	29.5	28.9	28.4	27.8	27.3	26.9	26.4										
64	31.1	30.4	29.8	29.2	28.6	28.0	27.4	26.9	26.4	25.9										
65	30.9	30.2	29.5	28.9	28.2	27.6	27.1	26.5	26.0	25.5	25.0	24.6	24.2	23.8	23.4	23.1	22.8	22.5	22.2	22.0
66	30.6	29.9	29.2	28.6	27.9	27.3	26.7	26.1	25.6	25.1	24.6	24.1	23.7	23.3	22.9	22.5	22.2	21.9	21.6	21.4
67	30.4	29.7	29.0	28.3	27.6	27.0	26.4	25.8	25.2	24.7	24.2	23.7	23.2	22.8	22.4	22.0	21.7	21.3	21.0	20.8
68	30.2	29.5	28.8	28.1	27.4	26.7	26.1	25.5	24.9	24.3	23.8	23.3	22.8	22.3	21.9	21.5	21.2	20.8	20.5	20.2
69	30.1	29.3	28.6	27.8	27.1	26.5	25.8	25.2	24.6	24.0	23.4	22.9	22.4	21.9	21.5	21.1	20.7	20.3	20.0	19.6
70	29.9	29.1	28.4	27.6	26.9	26.2	25.6	24.9	24.3	23.7	23.1	22.5	22.0	21.5	21.1	20.6	20.2	19.8	19.4	19.1
71	29.7	29.0	28.2	27.5	26.7	26.0	25.3	24.7	24.0	23.4	22.8	22.2	21.7	21.2	20.7	20.2	19.8	19.4	19.0	18.6
72	29.6	28.8	28.1	27.3	26.5	25.8	25.1	24.4	23.8	23.1	22.5	21.9	21.3	20.8	20.3	19.8	19.4	18.9	18.5	18.2
73	29.5	28.7	27.9	27.1	26.4	25.6	24.9	24.2	23.5	22.9	22.2	21.6	21.0	20.5	20.0	19.4	19.0	18.5	18.1	17.7
74	29.4	28.6	27.8	27.0	26.2	25.5	24.7	24.0	23.3	22.7	22.0	21.4	20.8	20.2	19.6	19.1	18.6	18.2	17.7	17.3
75	29.3	28.5	27.7	26.9	26.1	25.3	24.6	23.8	23.1	22.4	21.8	21.1	20.5	19.9	19.3	18.8	18.3	17.8	17.3	16.9
76	29.2	28.4	27.6	26.8	26.0	25.2	24.4	23.7	23.0	22.3	21.6	20.9	20.3	19.7	19.1	18.5	18.0	17.5	17.0	16.5
77	29.1	28.3	27.5	26.7	25.9	25.1	24.3	23.6	22.8	22.1	21.4	20.7	20.1	19.4	18.8	18.3	17.7	17.2	16.7	16.2
78	29.1	28.2	27.4	26.6	25.8	25.0	24.2	23.4	22.7	21.9	21.2	20.5	19.9	19.2	18.6	18.0	17.5	16.9	16.4	15.9
79	29.0	28.2	27.3	26.5	25.7	24.9	24.1	23.3	22.6	21.8	21.1	20.4	19.7	19.0	18.4	17.8	17.2	16.7	16.1	15.6
80	29.0	28.1	27.3	26.4	25.6	24.8	24.0	23.2	22.4	21.7	21.0	20.2	19.5	18.9	18.2	17.6	17.0	16.4	15.9	15.4
81	28.9	28.1	27.2	26.4	25.5	24.7	23.9	23.1	22.3	21.6	20.8	20.1	19.4	18.7	18.1	17.4	16.8	16.2	15.7	15.1
82	28.9	28.0	27.2	26.3	25.5	24.6	23.8	23.0	22.3	21.5	20.7	20.0	19.3	18.6	17.9	17.3	16.6	16.0	15.5	14.9
83	28.8	28.0	27.1	26.3	25.4	24.6	23.8	23.0	22.2	21.4	20.6	19.9	19.2	18.5	17.8	17.1	16.5	15.9	15.3	14.7
84	28.8	27.9	27.1	26.2	25.4	24.5	23.7	22.9	22.1	21.3	20.5	19.8	19.1	18.4	17.7	17.0	16.3	15.7	15.1	14.5
85	28.8	27.9	27.0	26.2	25.3	24.5	23.7	22.8	22.0	21.3	20.5	19.7	19.0	18.3	17.6	16.9	16.2	15.6	15.0	14.4
86	28.7	27.9	27.0	26.1	25.3	24.5	23.6	22.8	22.0	21.2	20.4	19.6	18.9	18.2	17.5	16.8	16.1	15.5	14.8	14.2
87	28.7	27.8	27.0	26.1	25.3	24.4	23.6	22.8	21.9	21.1	20.4	19.6	18.8	18.1	17.4	16.7	16.0	15.4	14.7	14.1
88	28.7	27.8	27.0	26.1	25.2	24.4	23.5	22.7	21.9	21.1	20.3	19.5	18.8	18.0	17.3	16.6	15.9	15.3	14.6	14.0
89	28.7	27.8	26.9	26.1	25.2	24.4	23.5	22.7	21.9	21.1	20.3	19.5	18.7	18.0	17.2	16.5	15.8	15.2	14.5	13.9
90	28.7	27.8	26.9	26.1	25.2	24.3	23.5	22.7	21.8	21.0	20.2	19.4	18.7	17.9	17.2	16.5	15.8	15.1	14.5	13.8
91	28.7	27.8	26.9	26.0	25.2	24.3	23.5	22.6	21.8	21.0	20.2	19.4	18.6	17.9	17.1	16.4	15.7	15.0	14.4	13.7
92	28.6	27.8	26.9	26.0	25.2	24.3	23.5	22.6	21.8	21.0	20.2	19.4	18.6	17.8	17.1	16.4	15.7	15.0	14.3	13.7
93	28.6	27.8	26.9	26.0	25.1	24.3	23.4	22.6	21.8	20.9	20.1	19.3	18.6	17.8	17.1	16.3	15.6	14.9	14.3	13.6
94	28.6	27.7	26.9	26.0	25.1	24.3	23.4	22.6	21.7	20.9	20.1	19.3	18.5	17.8	17.0	16.3	15.6	14.9	14.2	13.6
95	28.6	27.7	26.9	26.0	25.1	24.3	23.4	22.6	21.7	20.9	20.1	19.3	18.5	17.8	17.0	16.3	15.6	14.9	14.2	13.5
96	28.6	27.7	26.9	26.0	25.1	24.2	23.4	22.6	21.7	20.9	20.1	19.3	18.5	17.7	17.0	16.2	15.5	14.8	14.2	13.5
97	28.6	27.7	26.8	26.0	25.1	24.2	23.4	22.5	21.7	20.9	20.1	19.3	18.5	17.7	17.0	16.2	15.5	14.8	14.1	13.5
98	28.6	27.7	26.8	26.0	25.1	24.2	23.4	22.5	21.7	20.9	20.1	19.3	18.5	17.7	16.9	16.2	15.5	14.8	14.1	13.4
99	28.6	27.7	26.8	26.0	25.1	24.2	23.4	22.5	21.7	20.9	20.0	19.2	18.5	17.7	16.9	16.2	15.5	14.7	14.1	13.4
100	28.6	27.7	26.8	26.0	25.1	24.2	23.4	22.5	21.7	20.8	20.0	19.2	18.4	17.7	16.9	16.2	15.4	14.7	14.0	13.4
101	28.6	27.7	26.8	25.9	25.1	24.2	23.4	22.5	21.7	20.8	20.0	19.2	18.4	17.7	16.9	16.1	15.4	14.7	14.0	13.3
102	28.6	27.7	26.8	25.9	25.1	24.2	23.3	22.5	21.7	20.8	20.0	19.2	18.4	17.6	16.9	16.1	15.4	14.7	14.0	13.3
103	28.6	27.7	26.8	25.9	25.1	24.2	23.3	22.5	21.7	20.8	20.0	19.2	18.4	17.6	16.9	16.1	15.4	14.7	14.0	13.3
104	28.6	27.7	26.8	25.9	25.1	24.2	23.3	22.5	21.6	20.8	20.0	19.2	18.4	17.6	16.9	16.1	15.4	14.7	14.0	13.3
105	28.6	27.7	26.8	25.9	25.1	24.2	23.3	22.5	21.6	20.8	20.0	19.2	18.4	17.6	16.8	16.1	15.4	14.6	13.9	13.3
106	28.6	27.7	26.8	25.9	25.1	24.2	23.3	22.5	21.6	20.8	20.0	19.2	18.4	17.6	16.8	16.1	15.3	14.6	13.9	13.3
107	28.6	27.7	26.8	25.9	25.1	24.2	23.3	22.5	21.6	20.8	20.0	19.2	18.4	17.6	16.8	16.1	15.3	14.6	13.9	13.2
108	28.6	27.7	26.8	25.9	25.1	24.2	23.3	22.5	21.6	20.8	20.0	19.2	18.4	17.6	16.8	16.1	15.3	14.6	13.9	13.2
109	28.6	27.7	26.8	25.9	25.1	24.2	23.3	22.5	21.6	20.8	20.0	19.2	18.4	17.6	16.8	16.1	15.3	14.6	13.9	13.2
110	28.6	27.7	26.8	25.9	25.1	24.2	23.3	22.5	21.6	20.8	20.0	19.2	18.4	17.6	16.8	16.1	15.3	14.6	13.9	13.2
111	28.6	27.7	26.8	25.9	25.0	24.2	23.3	22.5	21.6	20.8	20.0	19.2	18.4	17.6	16.8	16.0	15.3	14.6	13.9	13.2
112	28.6	27.7	26.8	25.9	25.0	24.2	23.3	22.5	21.6	20.8	20.0	19.2	18.4	17.6	16.8	16.0	15.3	14.6	13.9	13.2
113	28.6	27.7	26.8	25.9	25.0	24.2	23.3	22.5	21.6	20.8	20.0	19.2	18.4	17.6	16.8	16.0	15.3	14.6	13.9	13.2
114	28.6	27.7	26.8	25.9	25.0	24.2	23.3	22.5	21.6	20.8	20.0	19.2	18.4	17.6	16.8	16.0	15.3	14.6	13.9	13.2
115	28.6	27.7	26.8	25.9	25.0	24.2	23.3	22.5	21.6	20.8	20.0	19.2	18.4	17.6	16.8	16.0	15.3	14.6	13.9	13.2

APPENDIX E. Life Expectancy Tables (continued)

TABLE II (continued)
(Joint Life and Last Survivor Expectancy)

AGES	75	76	77	78	79	80	81	82	83	84	85	86	87	88	89	90	91	92	93	94
75	16.5	16.1	15.8	15.4	15.1	14.9	14.6	14.4	14.2	14.0										
76	16.1	15.7	15.4	15.0	14.7	14.4	14.1	13.9	13.7	13.5										
77	15.8	15.4	15.0	14.6	14.3	14.0	13.7	13.4	13.2	13.0										
78	15.4	15.0	14.6	14.2	13.9	13.5	13.2	13.0	12.7	12.5										
79	15.1	14.7	14.3	13.9	13.5	13.2	12.8	12.5	12.3	12.0										
80	14.9	14.4	14.0	13.5	13.2	12.8	12.5	12.2	11.9	11.6										
81	14.6	14.1	13.7	13.2	12.8	12.5	12.1	11.8	11.5	11.2										
82	14.4	13.9	13.4	13.0	12.5	12.2	11.8	11.5	11.1	10.9										
83	14.2	13.7	13.2	12.7	12.3	11.9	11.5	11.1	10.8	10.5										
84	14.0	13.5	13.0	12.5	12.0	11.6	11.2	10.9	10.5	10.2										
85	13.8	13.3	12.8	12.3	11.8	11.4	11.0	10.6	10.2	9.9	9.6	9.3	9.1	8.9	8.7	8.5	8.3	8.2	8.0	7.9
86	13.7	13.1	12.6	12.1	11.6	11.2	10.8	10.4	10.0	9.7	9.3	9.1	8.8	8.6	8.3	8.2	8.0	7.8	7.7	7.6
87	13.5	13.0	12.4	11.9	11.4	11.0	10.6	10.1	9.8	9.4	9.1	8.8	8.5	8.3	8.1	7.9	7.7	7.5	7.4	7.2
88	13.4	12.8	12.3	11.8	11.3	10.8	10.4	10.0	9.6	9.2	9.9	8.6	8.3	8.0	7.8	7.6	7.4	7.2	7.1	6.9
89	13.3	12.7	12.2	11.6	11.1	10.7	10.2	9.8	9.4	9.0	8.7	8.3	8.1	7.8	7.5	7.3	7.1	6.9	6.8	6.6
90	13.2	12.6	12.1	11.5	11.0	10.5	10.1	9.6	9.2	8.8	8.5	8.2	7.9	7.6	7.3	7.1	6.9	6.7	6.5	6.4
91	13.1	12.5	12.0	11.4	10.9	10.4	9.9	9.5	9.1	8.7	8.3	8.0	7.7	7.4	7.1	6.9	6.7	6.5	6.3	6.2
92	13.1	12.5	11.9	11.3	10.8	10.3	9.8	9.4	8.9	8.5	8.2	7.8	7.5	7.2	6.9	6.7	6.5	6.3	6.1	5.9
93	13.0	12.4	11.8	11.3	10.7	10.2	9.7	9.3	8.8	8.4	8.0	7.7	7.4	7.1	6.8	6.5	6.3	6.1	5.9	5.8
94	12.9	12.3	11.7	11.2	10.6	10.1	9.6	9.2	8.7	8.3	7.9	7.6	7.2	6.9	6.6	6.4	6.2	5.9	5.8	5.6
95	12.9	12.3	11.7	11.1	10.6	10.1	9.6	9.1	8.6	8.2	7.8	7.5	7.1	6.8	6.5	6.3	6.0	5.8	5.6	5.4
96	12.9	12.2	11.6	11.1	10.5	10.0	9.5	9.0	8.5	8.1	7.7	7.3	7.0	6.7	6.4	6.1	5.9	5.7	5.5	5.3
97	12.8	12.2	11.6	11.0	10.5	9.9	9.4	8.9	8.5	8.0	7.6	7.3	6.9	6.6	6.3	6.0	5.8	5.5	5.3	5.1
98	12.8	12.2	11.5	11.0	10.4	9.9	9.4	8.9	8.4	8.0	7.6	7.2	6.8	6.5	6.2	5.9	5.6	5.4	5.2	5.0
99	12.7	12.1	11.5	10.9	10.4	9.8	9.3	8.8	8.3	7.9	7.5	7.1	6.7	6.4	6.1	5.8	5.5	5.3	5.1	4.9
100	12.7	12.1	11.5	10.9	10.3	9.8	9.2	8.7	8.3	7.8	7.4	7.0	6.6	6.3	6.0	5.7	5.4	5.2	5.0	4.8
101	12.7	12.1	11.4	10.8	10.3	9.7	9.2	8.7	8.2	7.8	7.3	6.9	6.6	6.2	5.9	5.6	5.3	5.1	4.9	4.7
102	12.7	12.0	11.4	10.8	10.2	9.7	9.2	8.7	8.2	7.7	7.3	6.9	6.5	6.2	5.8	5.5	5.3	5.0	4.8	4.6
103	12.6	12.0	11.4	10.8	10.2	9.7	9.1	8.6	8.1	7.7	7.2	6.8	6.4	6.1	5.8	5.5	5.2	4.9	4.7	4.5
104	12.6	12.0	11.4	10.8	10.2	9.6	9.1	8.6	8.1	7.6	7.2	6.8	6.4	6.0	5.7	5.4	5.1	4.8	4.6	4.4
105	12.6	12.0	11.3	10.7	10.2	9.6	9.1	8.5	8.0	7.6	7.1	6.7	6.3	5.0	5.6	5.3	5.0	4.8	4.5	4.3
106	12.6	11.9	11.3	10.7	10.1	9.6	9.0	8.5	8.0	7.5	7.1	6.7	6.3	5.9	5.6	5.3	5.0	4.7	4.5	4.2
107	12.6	11.9	11.3	10.7	10.1	9.6	9.0	8.5	8.0	7.5	7.1	6.6	6.2	5.9	5.5	5.2	4.9	4.6	4.4	4.2
108	12.6	11.9	11.3	10.7	10.1	9.5	9.0	8.5	8.0	7.5	7.0	6.6	6.2	5.8	5.5	5.2	4.9	4.6	4.3	4.1
109	12.6	11.9	11.3	10.7	10.1	9.5	9.0	8.4	7.9	7.5	7.0	6.6	6.2	5.8	5.5	5.1	4.8	4.5	4.3	4.1
110	12.6	11.9	11.3	10.7	10.1	9.5	9.0	8.4	7.9	7.4	7.0	6.6	6.2	5.8	5.4	5.1	4.8	4.5	4.3	4.0
111	12.5	11.9	11.3	10.7	10.1	9.5	8.9	8.4	7.9	7.4	7.0	6.5	6.1	5.7	5.4	5.1	4.8	4.5	4.2	4.0
112	12.5	11.9	11.3	10.6	10.1	9.5	8.9	8.4	7.9	7.4	7.0	6.5	6.1	5.7	5.4	5.0	4.7	4.4	4.2	3.9
113	12.5	11.9	11.2	10.6	10.0	9.5	8.9	8.4	7.9	7.4	6.9	6.5	6.1	5.7	5.4	5.0	4.7	4.4	4.2	3.9
114	12.5	11.9	11.2	10.6	10.0	9.5	8.9	8.4	7.9	7.4	6.9	6.5	6.1	5.7	5.3	5.0	4.7	4.4	4.1	3.9
115	12.5	11.9	11.2	10.6	10.0	9.5	8.9	8.4	7.9	7.4	6.9	6.5	6.1	5.7	5.3	5.0	4.7	4.4	4.1	3.9

Index

M

N

O

P

Q

R

S

T

U

W

Y

ABOUT THE AUTHOR

Seymour Goldberg is an attorney and a certified public accountant. He is the senior partner in the law firm of Goldberg & Ingber, P.C., in Garden City, New York, and has been practicing law since 1966.

Mr. Goldberg spends a great deal of his time in the areas of estate planning, estate taxation, and retirement distribution planning. He is a professor of law and taxation at the C.W. Post Campus of Long Island University, School of Professional Accountancy, College of Management. Mr. Goldberg has conducted workshops on retirement distribution planning throughout the United States. He was formerly associated with the Internal Revenue Service.

Mr. Goldberg is the recipient of outstanding discussion leader awards from both the American Institute of Certified Public Accountants and the Foundation for Accounting Education. He has been quoted extensively in the *New York Times*, *Forbes*, *Money Magazine*, and the *Boardroom Reports Tax Hotline*. Mr. Goldberg has taught many continuing professional education courses on taxation and pensions at the state and national levels and has taught continuing legal education courses for the New York State Bar Association.